The Power in Thinking
God's Way

Change Your Thinking...
Change Your Life

Bible Study

And do not be conformed to this world. But be
transformed by the renewing of your mind, that
you may prove what is that good and acceptable
and perfect will of God.
—Romans 12:2 (NKJV)

Judy Golightly

ISBN 978-1-64458-698-3 (paperback)
ISBN 978-1-64458-699-0 (digital)

Christian Faith Publishing, Inc.
832 Park Avenue
Meadville, PA 16335
www.christianfaithpublishing.com

All Scripture quotations contained in this study are taken from the New King James version, Thomas Nelson, Inc. © 1979. Other study reference guides used in this study include the following:

W.E. Vine Expository Dictionary of Biblical Words, Thomas Nelson, 1984.
Strong's Concordance, Dugan Publication, Gordansville, TN 38563.
Wyclijf Bible Commentary, PC Study Bible, Bible Soft Publishers, 1999.
Warren W. Wiersbe Commentary, Victor Books, Dunn SP Publications, 1978.
Microsoft Book Shelf Dictionary, 1995.
Thayer's Greek-English Lexicon
Webster's II New Riverside Dictionary, 1984, Berkley Publishing Group, 1984.

Printed in the United States of America

About the Author
The Power in Thinking God's Way Bible Study

Judy Golightly loves to share the word of God with others to encourage them. Saved on October 11, 1983, at a Baily Smith revival in Dallas, she has been studying God's Word ever since, serving as both a Precept student and leader.

Judy felt the Lord calling her to write on topics focusing on the renewal of the mind because He began to show her the truth of Proverbs 23:7, "For as a man thinks in his heart so is he," that many of her own problems were rooted in wrong thinking. She wrote *The Power in Thinking God's Way* to help people understand the importance of their thought lives and how to apply the Word of God in every situation of daily life and, through the power of the Holy Spirit, live a victorious, overcoming life.

Judy is living proof that there is power in thinking God's way. After completing her Bible study, she was diagnosed with breast cancer. Judy overcame the devastation of mastectomy and weeks of chemotherapy by choosing to think God's way, focusing and meditating on the Word of God and his promises, instead of her difficult circumstances. God used the months of writing *The Power in Thinking God's Way* to build a strong foundation under her that couldn't be shaken by the adversity of breast cancer.

God wants his children to be victorious overcomers in this world and that first starts with developing a victorious overcoming thought life. Judy is a living testimony to the power of God and His Word.

God has blessed Judy with a wonderful & supportive husband Bill. They have a beautiful daughter Keri and an awesome son in law Clint Poulter. Judy & Bill have been blessed with two precious grandchildren, Allison & Clinton.

They all reside in San Antonio, Texas.

Contents

Acknowledgments

I thank God for allowing me the opportunity to write *The Power in Thinking God's Way* and I pray He will use it for His glory and honor. I also wish to acknowledge the following:

Jackie Sciascia, for your encouragement, prayer, and careful study and review of each chapter.

Bill Golightly, for believing in me and this project and for your constant support and encouragement.

Women's Ministries Prayer Chain, for all your faithfulness to pray for the success of this study.

Keri Golightly, for your willingness to do each chapter of this study and for all the meaningful input you gave me. Thank you for continuing to believe in me even when I didn't believe in myself. I thank Pastor Dr. George H. Harris for his belief and endorsement of The Power in Thinking Gods Way.

Introduction

Our actions are a direct result of our thinking. Proverbs 23:7 says that our thoughts have the creative ability to determine what we become. Negative minds produce negative lives. Period. On the other hand, we can choose to build positive lives by changing the way we think.

I am not suggesting that all we have to do is think positive thoughts, and our lives will be perfect and trouble free. I believe all Christians should be positive because of who we are in Christ. As Christians, we have the power in thinking God's way available to us because we have the indwelling power of the Holy Spirit and the Word of God.

God has recorded His thoughts in the Holy Bible to help us understand how He thinks. He wants us to have His mind, His thoughts, and His viewpoint in every situation.

Right thinking—thinking that lines up with God's Word—is a vital necessity in a Christian's life. Our thoughts become our words. Our words become our deeds.

> Sow a thought, reap an action.
> Sow an action, reap a habit.
> Sow a habit, reap a character.
> Sow a character, reap a destiny.
> (Author Unknown)

Our thoughts set the course of our destiny. God desires us to enjoy a victorious life and to experience the power in thinking His way. A renewed mind is the link to experiencing a victorious thought life and living a transformed life.

> I beseech you therefore, brethren, by the mercies of God, that you present your bodies a living sacrifice, holy, acceptable to God, which is your reasonable service. And do not be conformed to this world, but be transformed by the renewing of your mind, that you may prove what is that good and acceptable and perfect will of God. (Romans 12:1–2)

In this passage, God exhorts us to surrender our lives to Him. One of the reasons why many Christians do not experience any real transformation is because we continue to depend upon our own natural thinking and reasoning rather than the mind of Christ. In Isaiah 55:8, we are told that our own natural thinking is opposite from God's thinking. God tells us that His thoughts are not our thoughts, and His ways are not our ways. In Proverbs 3:5, we are told to not lean on our own understanding but to trust the Lord with all our hearts, acknowledge Him in everything, and He promises to direct our paths.

God is calling Christians to a higher way of thinking by the renewing of our minds through the Word of God. The only way we can expect to know God's ways and His will for our lives is to study and meditate on His Word.

His Word is His will for us.

Another reason Christians are not living transformed lives is that we don't understand that we are in a spiritual battle with Satan and his demons. Satan's favorite battlefield is our minds. In 2 Corinthians 10:5, we are instructed to take every thought captive to the obedience of Christ. Any thought that provokes fear, worry, doubt, or confusion in us must be examined in the light of the truth of God's Word.

I lived a defeated life for many years. Yes, I was a Christian. I was saved and on my way to heaven. But I was living like a spiritual yo-yo. I was up one day and down the next. Often, my words and actions were not much different than those of an unbeliever. Eventually, I began to even doubt my salvation.

Finally, I decided to get serious with God. After much prayer and Bible study, He began to show me that my life was a mess because my mind was a mess. God took me to Proverbs 4:23, which tells us to guard our hearts with all diligence, for out of the heart flows the issues of life. Before this point, I never gave much thought to what I was thinking, let alone guarding what I was thinking. I soon realized that my thinking was conformed to the world and had become the devil's workshop.

When I acknowledged that this kind of thinking and life were not acceptable, God begun to do a new work in me. As I trusted in Him, stood on His Word, and rejected the devil's lies, I began to see a transformation taking place in my life. Today, I work daily to overcome negative thinking and to live a victorious life. And you can too.

It is my desire to see God transform your life as you learn and apply principles from His Word. Is this possible? *Yes!* Is it going to be easy? *No!* But will it be worth it? Absolutely!

Let this be the year that you overcome negative, "stinking" thinking.

How to Do This Study

This is a nine-week in-depth inductive Bible study. It is inductive in that you will be asked to read the Scripture to find the answer to your Bible study questions. You will find out for yourself what Scripture teaches, not just someone else's opinion. This is key in learning and understanding the Bible as it applies to you personally.

To get the most out of this study, it is important to take your time and study only one lesson at a time. Each chapter has five lessons, giving you one per day. Proceed through the lesson at your own pace. Do not run ahead and study several lessons per day. The study is designed to help you learn and apply truths from God's Word and to help you establish a personal daily walk with the Lord. Most importantly, pray before you begin and ask the Holy Spirit to open the eyes of your understanding.

Start each lesson by reading the Power Verse, then pray before you proceed. Learn to meditate on God's Word. Ponder upon each day's Power Meditation to help you hide God's Word in your heart.

You can do this as a personal bible study that you can do on your own or with a group that meet with once a week. The class will consist of a one-hour group discussion and a one-hour lecture. Depending on the size of the class, you may break up into small group settings of 8–10 people with a small group leader. I encourage you to attend the group discussions each week even if you have not completed all of your lesson. Obviously, you will benefit the most from the study if you finish your lesson each day, but if you have not been able to start or finish your lesson, you will still receive encouragement from the discussion, lecture, and fellowship.

The New King James version of the Bible has been utilized in this study; however, for your personal understanding, the New

International or New American Standard are equally good translations. You are about to start one of the most exciting journeys of your life. I pray God will use this study to transform you more and more into the image of Christ. As you begin, remember Jesus is your guide, and you have the greatest Bible study teacher in the universe—the Holy Spirit—living inside you. Part of His job is to teach you spiritual truth, which He will do as you trust and depend on Him.

The goal of this study is to help you pull down the strongholds of the mind to identify and overcome wrong thinking patterns, which produce problems in your life, and recognize where negative thinking has produced negative results in your life. You will learn how to overcome these by applying principles from God's Word. You will learn to stop believing the lies of the devil and learn to stand on God's Word as never before. Don't give up! Press on to the finish line, and you will be armed and dangerous!

Bible note pages are provided at the back of each chapter.

Chapter 1
The Importance of Our Thought Life

Day 1: Think About What You're Thinking About!
Power Verse: "For as he thinks in his heart, so is he." (Proverbs 23:7)

Welcome to Day One! The goal for the lesson this week is to encourage you to begin thinking about what you think about. We have three enemies in this life that attack our thinking: the devil, who is a liar and the father of lies; the flesh, which unfortunately will be with us until the Lord calls us home; and the world, which is an enemy of God and, therefore, our enemy. All three enemies work together to bombard our minds with thousands of thoughts that are often in opposition with God's plans for our lives.

If we are going to be successful in fulfilling God's purposes and plans for our lives, we must think right thoughts about who we are according to God's Word. God wants us to evaluate everything from His viewpoint. When difficult circumstances come into our lives, and we find ourselves going through adversity, it is easy to use natural reasoning and understanding to solve our problems instead of trusting God. Many of us have depended on natural reasoning for so long, it has become a habit. That is why, it is so important to study and meditate upon God's Word. God wants us to establish a new habit—to line up our thinking with His Word.

1. Read today's Power Verse, Proverbs 23:7, and write it out.
2. Look up the word heart in your concordance or Bible dictionary. Write down your thoughts. Is the writer of Proverbs speaking of the heart as an organ?
3. In your own words, write down what you think the verse is saying.
4. If our thoughts have the ability to determine what we become, what type of thinking in your life do you want to change?
5. In what areas of your thought life do you struggle the most? Write down the areas in which you want God to make changes.
6. Read Philippians 4:6–8. As it relates to your answer to question 5, how could you apply this verse to your thought life?
7. According to Philippians 4:6–8, what are the promises, conditions, and choices you must make in order to live a life free of anxious thoughts?

Power Challenge

How much time do I spend entertaining thoughts that are lies of the devil, selfish desires of the flesh or that are carnal or worldly? We can't always control what thoughts come into our minds, but we can control whether or not we are going to entertain those thoughts. Thoughts that provoke fear, worry, unbelief, confusion, and condemnation in us *must go*!

Power Meditation

"Set your mind on things above,_not on things on the earth" (Colossians 3:2).

Day 2: Guard Your Thought Life!
Power Verse: "Keep your heart with all diligence, for out of it spring the issues of life." (Proverbs 4: 23)

Heart is a term that includes the mind, emotions, and the will. Whatever we think about will show forth in our actions; therefore, we must guard our minds carefully. We know we have three enemies that affect our thinking: the devil, the world, and the flesh. All three will try to fill our minds with lies like: "I can't." "I might fail." "I'm not smart enough." "It's too hard." "What's the use?" Thoughts such as these will lead us into fear, worry, doubt, and unbelief if we don't take control of them.

God has an eternal purpose for His children. If we are to fulfill His purpose for our lives, it is vital that we begin to think like the redeemed children of God that we are.

In John 8:32, Jesus promises that the truth will set us free. Christians must know the truth—and that is found in the Word of God. In 2 Timothy 2:15, we are exhorted to be diligent in studying the Word of God so that we will not be ashamed but be able to rightly divide the word of truth.

Don't give place to a lie. Anything contrary to the Word of God is a lie. We can hear the truth and know the truth, but until we choose to practice the truth and become "doers" of the Word, we will not be the victorious overcomers that God desires us to be.

Today, we will examine several Scriptures that will help us see why and from what we are to guard our thinking.

1. Look up the words guard and diligence in a concordance or Bible dictionary. (A regular dictionary will work fine too.) Write down the definitions.

2. According to Proverbs 4:23, why should you guard your mind?

3. Of what in your life do you need to be watchful?

4. Diligence refers to perseverance, and guard suggests a defensive position in which you watch over carefully or take precautions. Are you diligently watching over your thought life? Or have you become passive in this area?

5. Satan wants to fill our minds with thoughts that oppose God's plans for our lives. Read Genesis 3:1–6. How is Satan described in verse 1? What was the first question Satan asked which caused Eve to have doubts? What lie did Satan speak?

Satan is using the same lies and tactics today. Nothing has changed. He tries to cause us to doubt the integrity of God. He wants us to believe the lie that God is withholding good things from us and that we ourselves can become like God. Satan is still as cunning as he was in the garden. He makes everything—in this case, food—look appealing so that it can't possibly be bad for us. Don't be fooled. God's ways are always best. Eve forgot how good God had been to her. Instead of focusing on how God had blessed her, she turned her eyes and focused on the only thing God told her she could not have.

6. Examine your own life. Ask God to help you identify areas where you are believing Satan's lies and are doubting God and His goodness. One of the best ways to identify wrong thinking is to look at how you respond in the midst of adversity or difficult circumstances. Where was your focus during that time? On the problem or on the Problem-Solver, our Heavenly Father?

7. Read 1 John 2:15–17. What four things are we warned to guard our minds against? What is the condition of the world? What is the promise for the one who does the will of the Father?

Colossians 3:2 says to set your mind on things above where Christ is seated and not on the things of this earth. God doesn't want us to fill our minds with temporal things of this world, which are passing away, but on things that have eternal consequences.

Power Challenge

How much time do you spend entertaining thoughts that are of temporal value? Turn your thinking over to God. Ask Him to help you think with an eternal perspective. Changing the way you think requires discipline. It will take diligence on your part, but God is faithful. He will give you the power to change those old thinking patterns and mindsets if we will do what 1 John 1:9 tells us to do.

Through prayer, confession and the determination to press on, God will help us to become victorious in our thought life.

Power Meditation

> "You will keep him in perfect peace, whose mind is stayed on You, because he trusts in You" (Isaiah 26:3).

Day 3: The Mind of Christ vs. the Mind of the Flesh

Power Verse: "Walk in the Spirit, and you shall not fulfill the lust of the flesh." (Galatians 5:16)

This week, we have been laying a foundation for the study we will cover over the next nine weeks. We have discovered how important our thinking is and how our thought patterns promote different types of behavior. We have learned that we have three enemies that attack our thinking, and therefore, we must guard our thoughts carefully. When we are born again, we don't automatically get new minds. We must renew our old minds to think a new way through God's Word and the indwelling power of the Holy Spirit. We are given a new Spirit—the Holy Spirit—at our rebirth, but unfortunately, God does not remove the old fleshly, carnal nature. God's desire for every Christian is to live a life led and controlled by the Spirit.

This is where the spiritual battle takes place in a believer's life. Galatians 5:17 says that the flesh lusts against the Spirit and the Spirit against the flesh, and these are contrary to one another so that you do not do the things that you wish. Sounds almost hopeless doesn't it? There is hope. We have God's promise that He who began a good work in us will be faithful to complete it (Philippians 1:6).

We serve a great God with great promises. He has given us His Word and has filled us with His Spirit so that we can't fail. We need to cooperate with the Holy Spirit by renewing our minds to think like God intended. In Isaiah 55:8–9, we are reminded that God's thoughts are not our thoughts and that His thoughts are higher than our thoughts. God wants us to attain a higher level of thinking.

Right thinking leads to right living.

If we are going to live a Spirit-controlled life, we must choose to exchange our old self-centered, fleshly thoughts for God's thoughts. How we think affects how we feel. How we feel influences our desires and will ultimately determine our actions. Today, we will look at the contrast between the mind of the Spirit and the mind of the flesh.

1. Read Romans 8:5–6. Where do you set your mind when you are walking in the Spirit?
2. What is the result of setting your mind on things of the Spirit?
3. What contrast does this passage show us?
4. What is the result of setting your mind on the things of the flesh?
5. Read Galatians 5:16–26. According to verse 16, what will walking by the Spirit enable you to do?
6. Make a list of the fruit that is manifested when we walk in the flesh.
7. Now make a list of the fruit that is manifested by walking by the Spirit.
8. As you review these lists, what do you hear God telling you?
9. Does this passage tell us how we can know if we're walking in the Spirit or in the flesh?
10. Do you think it is possible to go back and forth, walking in the Spirit and in the flesh? Explain why or why not.
11. Right thinking is a vital necessity for every believer. Our thoughts—right or wrong—bear fruit. I believe that each of us can look at the list in Galatians 5:16–26 and see our lives bearing fruit from the flesh and the Spirit. Many Christians try to improve the flesh when, in fact, the flesh will always be the flesh.

The most natural thing for the flesh to do is lust. Galatians 5:16 says that if we walk in the Spirit, we shall not fulfill the lust of the flesh. The desire may still be present, but by submitting to the power and control of the Holy Spirit, we will not carry out or fulfill the desires of the flesh. When we walk in the mind of the flesh, we will quench the power of the Holy Spirit. We need the power of the Holy Spirit if we are going to live a Spirit-controlled life and fulfill God's purposes for our lives. We cannot do the work of the Spirit in the energy of the flesh. We will burn out trying. Zechariah 4:6 says, "'Not by might nor by power, but by My Spirit,' says the Lord of hosts." Seek the Holy Spirit. He is your helper. With Him, you're never alone.

Power Challenge

On what do I spend most of my time meditating? Are my thoughts more self-centered? Or are they God-centered? How much time do I spend thinking and meditating on the past or the future instead of enjoying today and living in the present moment of right now?

Make Philippians 4:8 a habit: "Finally, brethren, whatever things are true, whatever things are noble, whatever things are just, whatever things are pure, whatever things are lovely, whatever things are of good report, if there is any virtue and if there is anything praiseworthy—meditate on these things."

When a bad thought pops into your mind, and you start having a bad thought day, ask yourself: Is what I am thinking true, noble, pure, just, lovely, praiseworthy? Don't give place in your thought life to Satan's lies. Diligently—not passively—guard your mind using the Sword of the Spirit, the Word of God.

It's a choice. The choice is yours to make. Choose to *choose* right thoughts.

Power Meditation

"Blessed is the man who walks not
in the counsel of the ungodly
but his delight is in the law of the Lord,
and in His law he meditates day and night.
He shall be like a tree planted by the rivers of water,
that brings forth its fruit in its season,
whose leaf also shall not wither;
and whatever he does shall prosper" (Psalm 1:1–3).

Day 4: The Mind of Faith vs. the Mind of the Flesh

Power Verse: "But I without faith it is impossible to please Him, for he who comes to God must believe that He is, and that He is a rewarder of those who diligently seek Him." (Hebrews 11:6)

We have been looking at the importance of our thought lives. We have learned that our thinking will ultimately determine what we become and that we need to guard our thoughts against the lies of the devil and any type of thinking that is contrary to God's Word. We have also discovered how our thoughts produce fruit. Good thinking produces good fruit; bad thinking produces bad fruit.

Today, we will look at how important our thinking is to our faith. Romans 1:17 says that the just shall live by faith, and our Power Verse today tells us that it is impossible to please God without faith.

God intends for the Christian to live and walk by faith. Romans 14:23 says that whatever is not of faith is sin, and we need to deal with it as sin. Since our thinking leads to words and then to actions, we could stop a lot of sin in our lives if we would stop the thoughts in our minds that are not of God.

How we handle trials and adversity in our lives is a clue to the kind of faith we have. When trials come, do you trust God and stand on His promises? Or do you worry, fret, and become fearful?

Today, we are going to look into the Word of God and examine whether we are walking by faith or by our feelings (the flesh). We will also look at how our thinking determines the quality of our faith.

1. In a Bible dictionary, look up the word faith, and write down the definition.
2. Does walking by faith involve our minds only? Or does faith also involve our will and emotions?
3. How does Hebrews 11:1 define faith?
4. What should the object of our faith be according to Hebrews 11:6?
5. According to Romans 10:17, how do we get faith?
6. Examine your faith walk. Who or what is the object or focus of your faith?

7. Are you able to believe God for things you cannot see in the natural?

   We will never have great faith apart from the Word of God. Faith and the Word of God go hand-in-hand. Faith is believing God will do what He promised He will do in spite of our feelings, circumstances, or consequences. Spend some time meditating on Hebrews 11 in its entirety. Make a list of the Old Testament characters mentioned and what it says about each one's faith. This exercise will build your own faith in the process, because as we have seen, faith comes by hearing or reading the Word of God.

   Having faith in faith itself is worthless. The object of true biblical faith is God and God alone. Faith in God enables us to see the invisible and to believe God for what we don't have yet. God wants our thinking, our words, and our actions to line up with His Word. He wants us to have His thought and viewpoint in every situation. Walking by faith means that I am going to believe what God says about me and not what others—or I— think about the situation. When I begin to deal with every situation that comes into my life from the mind of faith, it will free me from being controlled by my feelings. Then and only then can the Holy Spirit truly control my life.

8. Read Numbers 13:1, 2, 27, 33 and 14:6–8. What had God told Moses in verses 1 and 2? Who gave the land to the children of Israel?

9. How did they describe the land God gave them in verses 27–33?

10. What was the response of Joshua and Caleb in Numbers 14:6–9?

11. Where did the Israelites place their focus? What does this tell us about their thinking toward God?

12. In contrast, where did Joshua and Caleb place their focus? What does this tell us about their thinking toward God?

13. Where do you place your focus when you have just received a bad report?

The children of Israel had what I call "grasshopper" mentality. They focused on the giants in the land instead of the Great and Awesome God, who had performed so many miracles in their lives. God had promised them this land. And He promised He would drive back their enemies, but they chose not to believe God but to believe in their circumstances. Joshua and Caleb, on the other hand, demonstrated great faith because they kept their focus on God. They knew God was faithful to do what He promised. How about you? Do you see God as the Giant He is? Or do you suffer with "grasshopper" mentality that makes God too small to tackle the giants in your life?

Power Challenge

Meditate on the attributes of God this week. Read Psalm 18, and make a list of God's attributes and His promises. Choose to meditate on who God is. When opportunities arise that cause you to fear or get angry, run to God, who has promised to be your rock and refuge. Choose to walk with the mind of faith instead of the mind of the flesh. The walk of faith is a choice that you must make.

Power Meditation

"For we walk by faith, not by sight" (2 Corinthians 5: 7).

Day 5: Right Thinking Will Lead to Right Praying

Power Verse: "And all things, whatever you ask in prayer, believing, you will receive." (Matthew 21:22)

Yesterday, we learned that the Christian walk is a walk of faith. Faith is believing God in spite of feelings or circumstances. If we ever expect to have a healthy prayer life, we must get hold of the truth that the just shall live by faith, and without faith, it is impossible to please God. We are to place our faith in awesome, mighty God, who is faithful to keep His promises and to perform His Word. As discussed yesterday, "Faith comes by hearing, and hearing by the Word of God" (Romans 10: 17). To have a powerful faith walk, we must study and meditate on God's Word and act upon what it says to do.

The same is true if we are going to have a powerful prayer life. The prayer of faith is praying in agreement with what God's Word says. If we don't get into the Word on a daily basis, we will not experience a powerful prayer life. Instead, we will be so led by our feelings that our prayers will flow from our feelings instead of our faith. The devil loves for you and I to focus on our feelings because when we do, he knows our faith will be greatly hindered and our prayers weakened.

I have experienced this over and over in my prayer life. Perhaps, I have said things or my actions were less than godly in a particular situation. The devil begins to put guilt and condemnation on me. I begin to believe that God is mad at me and certainly will not listen to my prayers.

What is taking place? My walk is based on my feelings and not at all by faith. Faith says that God loves me unconditionally, that Christ paid the price for my sins and according to Hebrews 4:16, I can come boldly and confidently into God's throne room to obtain mercy and grace in my time of need.

1 John 1:9 says that if I will confess my sins before God, He is faithful and just to forgive me and to cleanse me of all unrighteousness. When we line up our thinking with the Word of God and pray accordingly, we will begin to see major breakthroughs in our life. But as long as we walk by our feelings and emotions, we will never get the devil off our backs. Walking by feelings instead of by faith in God's promises will keep us in a constant state of confusion, and we will have a hit-or-miss prayer life.

Today, we want to examine God's Word and identify thinking that will attack our faith and destroy our prayer lives.

1. Look up the word *believe* in your Bible dictionary. Write your insights about this word.
2. What is the opposite of believe?

3. Faith and believing go hand-in-hand. Read Matthew 13:58. What kept Jesus from doing mighty works?

4. Write the definition for unbelief.

5. One reason we don't see the mighty works of God more often in our lives is unbelief. Faith involves the will. If we perceive a particular principle from God's Word to be true and yet choose to not act upon it, that is unbelief. Unbelief is disobedience.

6. Read Matthew 17:17–20. What did Jesus call an enemy of our faith?

7. How does Jesus describe faith and its power in this passage?

8. Read Matthew 14: 26–31. How does Jesus describe Peter's faith? What did Jesus say was the enemy of Peter's faith?

9. Just like Peter, when we take our eyes off Jesus and start looking at the storms in our lives, we begin to doubt God. Our faith becomes weak and we falter.

10. Read Mark 11: 23–26. What does Jesus say that you and I must do to receive what we pray for?

11. According to these verses, what can this kind of prayer accomplish?

12. What mountains do you have in your life at this time? Do you believe God can move them?

13. Read James 1:5–8. James is writing to Jewish Christians who are being persecuted with many trials. List the things we are to do in prayer when we go through trials and adversity. How is a doubting person described in these verses? What results from doubt?

14. Doubt will shut down our faith and render our prayer life powerless. Doubt—especially doubt that is habitual—leads us into discouragement, despair, and depression. Doubt leads to unbelief, which is disobedience to God. Doubt is walking in two minds or trying to stand in two ways. Doubt always brings uncertainty as to which way to take. It produces anxious thoughts that keep us vacillating between hope and fear. Doubt comes from thoughts that directly oppose the Word of God. That is why it is so important

to know the Word. Only then will we recognize when the devil is lying to us. Satan knows how dangerous we are when we pray with a mind filled with faith, so he attacks us with doubt and unbelief. Recognize doubt for what it is and know where it comes from. Reject it in the name of Jesus and ask God to empower you by the Holy Spirit to walk with the mind of faith.

Power Challenge

Ask God to shine the searchlight of His Holy Spirit upon your life and reveal any areas in which you might be walking in doubt and unbelief. As God shows them to you, write them down. Go to the Lord in prayer. Confess them as sin to God, and as 1 John 1:9 promises, God will forgive you and cleanse you of all unrighteousness. Turn your thinking over to God and tell Him that by His power, you are determined to press on to victory!

Well! You have finished the first chapter. You are on the road to victory!

Power Meditation

> "Call to me, and I will answer you, and show you great and mighty things, which you do not know" (Jeremiah 33:3).

_____

_____

_____

_____

_____

_____

_____

_____

_____

_____

_____

_____

_____

_____

_____

_____

_____

_____

_____

_____

_____

_____

_____

_____

_____

Chapter 2
The Mind Is the Battlefield

Day 1: Pick Up Your Weapons

Power Verse: "For though we walk in the flesh, we do not war according to the flesh. For the weapons of our warfare are not carnal but mighty in God for pulling down strongholds, casting down arguments and every high thing that exalts itself against the knowledge of God, bringing every thought into captivity to the obedience of Christ." (2 Corinthians 10:3–5)

Today, we are going to study our Power Verse to get a clearer understanding of its meaning and how we can apply it to our lives. Bible studies should never be just a process of taking in a lot of information but a means by which transformation is taking place in our lives. That is why applying what we learn is vital to transforming our lives.

Information + Application = Transformation

1. Read 2 Corinthians 10:3–5. Where is the warfare taking place?
2. Describe the weapons that we are to use in this battle.
3. What are these weapons able to do?
4. According to verse 5, how are we to deal with strongholds of the mind, arguments, and thoughts that exalt themselves against the knowledge of God?
5. Think about your own life and make a list of thoughts that cause a lot of doubt and confusion, thereby stealing your joy and peace.

6. Let's summarize these verses:

- We are engaged in a spiritual war.
- Our enemies are Satan and his demonic forces.
- The mind is the battlefield.
- The devil is working to establish strongholds in our minds. He offers reasoning and arguments to work out his plans, which are in direct opposition to God's plans.
- The battle will not be won with fleshly weapons, but with divine weapons "mighty in God."

7. Satan attempts to defeat us with all types of lies. John 8:44 calls Satan "a liar and the father of it." As mentioned throughout this study, it is important to know the Word of God. Only then will we recognize when Satan is coming at us with his lies of hopelessness, criticism, and suspicions. These thoughts are not from our Heavenly Father, so take them captive in obedience to Christ.

   Don't get discouraged, my friend. We have promises from God in 1 John 4:4 that "He who is in you is greater than he who is in the world." God did not leave us orphans but has sealed us with the Holy Spirit until the day of redemption. When we use His Word—the Sword of the Spirit—to fight Satan, he and his lies are sliced and diced and made useless. Remember: Satan's greatest tool is a lie. Our greatest tool is truth from God's Word.

Power Challenge

When Satan fills your mind with thoughts that oppose God's plans for your life, get into the habit of saying, "These are not my Father's thoughts, and I refuse to receive them."

Quote God's promise out loud, and praise God for what He is doing in your life. When you speak God's Word, visualize that you are speaking swords out of your mouth that are expelling the darkness around you. Again, the choice is yours. You can choose to be passive in guarding your mind, or you can choose to diligently guard your mind. Which one do you choose?

Power Meditation

> "We also glory in tribulations, Knowing that tribulation produces perseverance; And perseverance, character, and character, hope" (Romans 5: 3).

Day 2: Bringing Thoughts Captive to the Obedience of Christ

Power Verse: "'For I know the thoughts that I think toward you,' says the Lord, 'thoughts of peace and not of evil, to give you a future and a hope.'" (Jeremiah 29: 11)

According to Jeremiah 29:11, God has a plan for our lives, a plan that includes peace, hope, and a future. The devil tries to fill our minds with thoughts that oppose God's plans for us. Many Christians have believed the lies of the enemy for so long that they have built up strongholds in their minds.

Today, we want to understand strongholds and how we can bring destructive thoughts captive to obedience to Christ.

The original Greek word for stronghold is *ochuroma*, which means to fortify by holding safely. To paraphrase Thayer's Greek-English Lexicon, a stronghold is what one uses to fortify and defend a personal belief, idea, or opinion against outside opposition. Simply put, a stronghold is the fortification around and a defense of what you believe, even if what you believe is a lie.

If you have believed and bought into the devil's lies, you will fight to protect those lies. Perhaps he has convinced you that you are unworthy, insignificant, not smart enough to accomplish big things in your life. This is not what God's Word says about you, but if you choose to believe those lies, then Satan has won this battle in your mind.

A perfect example is the anorexic woman. She doesn't eat because she believes the lie that she is too fat when, in fact, she has become dangerously thin. Her doctor, family, or friends can say nothing that will convince her of this life-threatening disorder. She has chosen to believe this lie of the devil, and her mind has erected strongholds that protect the lie even to death.

1. According to 2 Corinthians 10:5–6, what type of thoughts should we bring captive to the obedience of Christ?

2. Does this definition ever describe your thinking? If so, write down your insights.

3. Verse 5 tells us to bring captive to the obedience of Christ any thought that exalts itself against the knowledge of God. In Isaiah, we find the account of Lucifer's fall. Read Isaiah 14:12–14. What caused Lucifer to fall?

4. Lucifer wanted to be like God and exalt himself above the throne of God. Read Genesis 3:1–6. With what lie was the devil trying to trick Eve?

5. Examine your own life for any self-centered, self-sufficient, self-seeking, and selfish thinking. This type of thinking is focused on self and not on God and exalts itself against the knowledge of God. It is thinking that says self must always be in control instead of God. Only God has control over everything. Don't remove God's rightful place in your life by trying to exalt yourself above His control. Stop trying to play God!

6. Second Corinthians 10:5 says we are to take all thoughts captive to the obedience of Christ. In a dictionary, look up the words *captive* and *obedience*, and write the definitions here.

7. How is Christ described in John 1:1–4 and 14?

8. We are to take these thoughts captive because they are the enemy's thoughts. We are to take captive any thought that is contrary to the Word of God, contrary to His personality, character and nature. We are to capture and take prisoner any thought that provokes confusion, fear, worry, doubt, unbelief, and selfishness and bring it under the authority of the Word of God. The Word of God is the Sword of the Spirit and part of the armor that Paul instructs us to put on in Ephesians 6:17. A sword kept in its sheath is

powerless; it is of no defensive value. Only when the sword is taken out of the sheath does it become an effective and powerful weapon. This is also true with the Word of God. Its power comes when we choose to receive it, believe it, and act upon it. The Word of God is our defensive weapon against Satan's lies.

9. How has God spoken to you today?

Power Challenge

Pray and ask God to show you any patterns of thinking or mindsets contrary to His Word that are present in your life. In the power of the Holy Spirit, pick up the sword of the Spirit and begin taking those thoughts prisoner under the authority of God's Word. As God to help you preserve and choose to press on to victory. Paul said in Philippians 3:13–14 that we are to forget those things that are behind us—past mistakes, past failures, past regrets—and press on to what is ahead. Press on to the prize in the upward call of God in Christ Jesus.

Don't let the devil pull you back into the past. Forget any regrets and press, pray, and praise God for the prize!

Power Meditation

"And let us not grow weary while doing good, for in due season we shall reap if we do not lose heart" (Galatians 6:9).

Day 3: Armed and Dangerous
Power Verse: "Finally, my brethren, be strong in the Lord and in the power of His might. Put on the whole armor of God, that you may be able to stand against the wiles of the devil." (Eph. 6:10–11)

In heaven, we will wear robes, but while on earth as believers, we must wear armor. So far, we have discovered that we are engaged in a spiritual battle with Satan and his demonic forces. One of the primary locations for this battle is in our minds. These forces of evil invade our territory every day with wicked intentions of destroying us. From studying 2 Corinthians 10:3–4, we know that to win this battle, our weapons are not fleshly or carnal but are of a divine nature. They are mighty in God. Hallelujah!

The rest of the week, we will look at the armor that we are commanded to put on so that we can stand against the wiles of the devil. Obviously, in a physical sense, we aren't going to walk around wearing metal armor. Our armor is spiritual, and we need to understand what it is and how to put it to use in our lives.

1. Read Ephesians 6:10–20. According to verses 10–11, what three things must we do to stand against the wiles of the devil?

2. "Finally, my brethren, be strong in the Lord." This is an imperative—a command that denotes continuous action. We must keep on being strong in the Lord. Why? Because our enemy is too strong and too wicked for us to be able to stand against him in our own flesh.

3. Look up the word *wiles* in the dictionary. Record your insights.

4. The devil has a well-planned strategy. He knows us very well, and he knows our areas of weakness, which become his primary targets. Sometimes we think our battle is with our neighbor, our spouse, our children, or our friends. But according to verse 12, our battle is with what?

5. We are in a battle with wicked and immoral cosmic powers. Since our weapons are mighty in God and we have been commanded to be "strong in the Lord and in the power of His might," we need to evaluate our weapons and see how we are to use them. Read verse 14. What is the first piece of armor we must put on?

6. Read John 14:6. What does Jesus say about truth?

7. Read John 8:31–32. What does Jesus say that knowing the truth will do?

8. When we evaluate everything that comes into our life on the basis of the truth of God's Word, we will be set free from believing the lies of the devil. Practicing the truth of the Word of God, I know the good news that Jesus Christ has paid my sin debt in full. I am forgiven, and I am eternally secure in Him.

9. According to verse 14, what is the second piece of armor we are to put on?

10. Read 2 Corinthians 5:21. What does this verse say about righteousness?

11. Read Romans 3:10–11. How does God view our righteousness?

12. How do we obtain righteousness according to Romans 3:23, 26?

13. When the devil hits you with lies that you are not good enough, holy enough, or righteous enough, you simply stand on the truth of God's Word. You can tell him in no uncertain terms that your righteousness was purchased at Calvary through the precious blood of Jesus. You now wear Jesus's robe of righteousness, which gives you right standing before your Father in heaven.

That's all for today. I know you have had a lot of reading and studying to do. I pray that God will reward your diligence. We will pick up tomorrow on the remaining pieces of armor that we are to wear so that we can be victorious in life's battles.

Power Challenge

Examine your life. Is there any anger, bitterness, resentment, or unforgiveness? These can become serious strongholds and targets that give the devil access into our lives. If you do not forgive, you are a prisoner of your own strongholds. Bitterness, anger, and resentment are toxic to the soul and will lead to destructive thought patterns that ultimately lead to a destructive lifestyle. If you identify any of these destructive mindsets in your life, confess them to God and ask Him for forgiveness, healing and, restoration. Therefore, if the Son makes you free, you shall be free indeed."(John 8:36)

Power Meditation

> "When the enemy comes in like a flood, the Spirit of the Lord will lift up a standard against him" (Isaiah 59:19).

Day 4: Victors, Not Victims

Power Verse: "Yet in all these things we are more than conquerors through Him who loved us." (Romans 8:37)

We are continuing today to look at the spiritual armor we must wear in order to stand against the wiles of the devil. In an earlier lesson, you looked up the definition for wiles. Webster's defines wile as a "stratagem or trick intended to entrap or deceive. It is deceitful, cunning guile with the idea to seduce." The devil has a strategy, a well-laid plan designed to deceive and seduce you and I. But he will have problems carrying out his evil scheme when we put on the spiritual armor of God, and we seek to continually be strong in the Lord and in the power of His might.

Romans 8:37 says that "we are more than conquerors through Him who loved us." God intends for us to be victors, not victims. God's Word says that "He who is in you is greater than he who is in the world." Our weapons are divine and mighty through God. We cannot fail if we are trusting, leaning, and depending on El Shaddai because His very name in Hebrew tells us that our God is the All-Sufficient One. We serve a God who is all-knowing, all-powerful, God Almighty.

Trust today in His sovereignty. Romans 8:31 says that "if God is for us, who can be against us?" Take comfort in knowing that God is on your side, and He has promised to never leave us nor forsake us.

Today, we will examine the remaining armor discussed in Ephesians 6:15–18.

1. According to verse 15, what are we to put on our feet?
2. The gospel is the Good News, and we know that Jesus is the Prince of Peace—He is our peace. Read 1 Corinthians 3:9–15. On what foundation should we build and stand?
3. These verses tell us that we can build with gold, silver, and precious stones, which represent the quality of a life built with imperishable materials. We can also build with wood, hay, and straw, which represent a life built with perishable materials.
4. According to 1 Corinthians 3:13–15, when we stand before the Judgment Seat of Christ, what will result from our choice of building material?
5. What does verse 15 make clear about our salvation?
6. As we build on Christ as our foundation, we have peace with God because Ephesians 2:14 says that Jesus is our peace. The devil can't shake a life which has Christ as its foundation. Jesus is our rock.
7. Read Ephesians 6:16. What is the shield of faith able to do?
8. Based on what we have studied in a recent lesson on faith, how do you think carrying the shield of faith will quench the devil's fiery darts?
9. How is faith defined in Hebrews 11:1?
10. What does 2 Corinthians 5:7 instruct us to do?
11. One of the greatest enemies to our faith, besides doubt, is our feelings. We are not called to walk by our feelings but by faith. Faith believes God in spite of feelings or circumstances. As long as we are walking by our feelings, we will never escape the fiery arrows of the devil. It is only when we walk by faith that the devil's arrows will be quenched.
12. What two pieces of armor are mentioned in Ephesians 6:17?
13. The enemy will attack you in the area of your salvation. He loves nothing more than to get us to doubt our salvation. He uses arrows filled with lies, then he whispers in our ears that we can lose our salvation or that we are not eternally secure. This is when we must pick up the Sword of the Spirit and stand firm on what God tells us through His

Word. Don't stand on what you feel or think but firmly on what God's Word says.

14. Let's look at some Scriptures that discuss salvation. Read Ephesians 2:8–9. How are we saved according to this verse?

15. According to Ephesians 1:7, what does the blood of Jesus provide for those who believe?

16. Read Ephesians 1:13–14. What happened the moment you trusted Christ?

17. How long does this verse say you and I will be sealed with the Holy Spirit?

18. Read John 3:15–16. What do these verses teach about salvation?

How long is our salvation?

19. Our salvation is everlasting. It is eternal. It can't end, and we can't lose it. Don't live in limbo regarding your salvation! Instead, rejoice! Your name has been written in the Lamb's Book of Life. Amen.

Power Challenge

Begin appropriating your spiritual armor today. Put what you have been learning into practice. Regardless of the circumstances you are now facing—whether they are physical, financial, spiritual, or emotional—pray and ask God to give you His strength and His wisdom. Practice walking in the truth of God's Word that Jesus is your righteousness. Choose to walk by faith and not by your feelings. Stand firmly on God's Word and meditate on it. Don't focus on your problems. Rejoice in your salvation. We have been delivered out of darkness into His marvelous light.

Power Meditation

"No temptation has overtaken you except such as is common to man; but God is faithful, who will

39

not allow you to be tempted beyond what you are able, but with the temptation will also make the way of escape, that you may be able to bear it" (1 Corinthians 10:13).

Day 5: The Privilege, Power, and Promise of Prayer

Power Verse: "Then He spoke a parable to them, that men always ought to pray and not lose heart." (Luke 18:1)

We will finish chapter 2 by looking at two powerful weapons we have in our arsenal as seen in Ephesians 6:17–18, the Word of God and prayer.

The Bible is the inspired Word of God. In 2 Timothy 3:16–17, we find that "all Scripture is given by the inspiration of God, and is profitable for doctrine, for reproof, for correction, for instruction in righteousness, that the man of God may be complete, thoroughly equipped for every good work."

God wants us to become "Word Thinkers" and not "World Thinkers." Unfortunately, many Christians have their thinking shaped by the world's values and perspectives—not by God's Word. The Word of God is what fuels our faith because faith comes by hearing and hearing by the Word of God. The Word of God instructs us in how we are to pray and, most certainly, the Word of God should be an integral part of our prayers.

Prayer is the lifeline between believers and our Heavenly Father. Prayer is communication with God. In Matthew 6, we have the account of Jesus talking to His disciples about prayer. It is here that Jesus gave us the Lord's Prayer. The purpose of the Lord's Prayer was to teach His disciples how to pray and to show us that God is our Heavenly Father and that He desires to have a personal and intimate relationship with His children. Yes, as believers in Jesus Christ, we become children of God.

As God's children, we should look at prayer as an awesome privilege. But so many times, we make prayer our last option. It's our last resort. Instead of praying like we ought to pray, many Christians lose heart and give up. Jesus teaches us the pattern for praying in Matthew 6:9–13. If Christians would get into the discipline of daily prayer and use the Lord's Prayer as a pattern, they would see God answer more of their prayers and experience greater victories in their lives.

Prayer is an act of faith. It shows our dependence on God. Remember, we have an enemy who is roaming around like a roaring lion, seeking people to devour. So we need to be vigilant in prayer.

Let's look at the power of God's Word and the privilege, power, and promises of prayer.

1. How does Hebrews 4:12 describe the Word of God?
2. List everything that God says about His Word in Isaiah 55:11.
3. As we think of the Word of God as our only defensive weapon, summarize Hebrews 4:12 and Isaiah 55:11, describing how powerful the weapon of the Word is.
4. Read the account of Jesus being tempted by the devil in Luke 4:1–13. What did the devil use to entice Jesus to bow down and worship him?
5. What weapon did Jesus use to combat the devil's devices?

What was the result?

6. When Satan tried to tempt Jesus in the wilderness, he failed because Jesus was totally surrendered to the Father's will. He resisted Satan by using the Sword of the Spirit— the Word of God. If Jesus, who was God in the flesh, used the Word of God to defeat Satan, then how much more important is it for you and I to use the Word of God to overcome the devil?
7. Read James 4:7. How are you and I told to resist the devil?

What is the promise if we do what the Word instructs us to do?

8. If we are going to resist the devil, we must do it as we are submitted to God. To try and resist the devil in our own strength without being submitted to God would be foolish and even dangerous. It is only as we are submitted to God that we are empowered by Him. Remember Ephesians

6:10 says to "be strong in the Lord and in the power of His might." If there is no surrender, there will be no power. To submit means to surrender to God's authority, supremacy, and His rulership over your life.

9. Prayer is one of our greatest privileges as Christians. Prayer brings the power we need to fulfill God's purposes in our lives. Read the twentieth chapter of 2 Chronicles. Jehoshaphat was in a battle with the people of Moab and Ammon. Jehoshaphat feared because he knew that his power was limited against this great multitude of people. What did Jehoshaphat do according to verse 3?

10. How did Jehoshaphat pray to God in verses 6–9? What did he focus on?

11. Jehoshaphat obviously knew the Word of God and the character of God, which is why his prayer was so powerful. He reminded God of the fact that God was sovereign, mighty, and powerful and that no one could stand against Him. He also reminded God of His faithfulness to the descendants of Abraham. We see evidence of Jehoshaphat's great faith in verse 9, when he is assured that God will see their affliction and hear their prayer and save them.

12. As a result of this great prayer of power and faith, what did God promise to do for them in verses 14–17?

13. What was their part in this battle?

14. How has God spoken to you today?

15. You have studied each piece of spiritual armor this week. Beside each one, write down how you are going to apply it in your life to overcome the lies of the devil.

Belt of Truth
Breastplate of Righteousness
Gospel Shoes of Peace
Shield of Faith
Helmet of Salvation
Sword of the Spirit
Prayer

Power Challenge

What a wonderful promise that the battle is not ours but the Lord's! The next time you have a crisis in your life, remember Jehoshaphat's prayer. Stand confidently on the Word of God and pray God's attributes and character. Remind Him of how mighty and powerful He is and thank Him ahead of time for His answer to your prayer. In the meantime, rest in God's promise that the battle is not yours but His. Simply position yourself in Christ, on the promises. Stand still and see the salvation of the Lord. Claim His promise. Do not fear or be dismayed, for the Lord is with you!

Power Meditation

> "But now, thus says the Lord, who created you and He who formed you 'Fear not, for I have redeemed you; I have called you by your name; you are Mine. When you pass through the waters, I will be with you; and through the rivers, they shall not overflow you. When you walk through the fire, you shall not be burned, nor shall the flame scorch you" (Isaiah 43:1–2).

Chapter 3
The Renewed Mind:
A Vital Necessity

Day 1: The Answer

Power Verse: "Do not be conformed to this world, but be transformed by the renewing of your mind, that you may prove what is that good and acceptable and perfect will of God." (Romans 12:2)

A renewed mind is our link to being transformed into the image of Christ and experiencing the power in thinking God's way. Many Christians do not understand the importance of a renewed mind, and as a result, their values and perspective are more influenced by their own natural thinking and human reasoning than by God's Word.

In Proverbs 3:5–6, we are instructed to "trust in the Lord with all your heart and lean not on your own understanding; in all your ways acknowledge Him, and He shall direct your paths."

I am sure that most Christians are familiar with this passage of Scripture, yet we don't put its instructions into practice. Many of us have depended on our own natural reasoning and human understanding for so long that it has become a habit. You may ask, "Well, didn't God give me a mind with which to think and make decisions?"

God gave us minds, and He expects us to use them. However, He intends that our minds be renewed to think the way He thinks so that when we make decisions, we will make them from God's viewpoint and perspective and based on His wisdom.

We need to keep our understanding in check with the Word of God. Proverbs 14:12 says, "There is a way which seems right to a man, but its end is the way of death." It is important that the Word of God directs our thinking because whoever or whatever directs our thinking will direct our lives as well. We will spend time in this chapter getting a thorough understanding of how we can renew our minds and enjoy transformed lives. Remember one thing:

If there is no mind change, there will be no life change.

1. Read Romans 12:1–2. How are we to make our bodies?
2. In your own words, what do you believe verse 1 means?
3. What two things are we commanded to do in verse 2?
4. According to verse 2, why are we commanded to do this?
5. To get a good understanding of what this passage of Scripture is teaching, let's look up several words in a Bible or Webster's dictionary. Please record your definitions and insights to the following words.

   World
   Conform or Conformed
   Transform or Transfigure
   Renew

6. In your own words, what do you think verse 2 is instructing us to do?

Is this a one-time action or a continuing process?

7. As you look at Romans 12:1–2, notice that the first command that we are given is to a surrendered life. The second command, in verse 2, is to not be conformed to the world but be transformed by the renewing of our minds. How do you think these verses are linked together?

Power Challenge

Prayerfully, ask God to reveal areas in your life that you need to surrender to Him. God wants us to submit our thoughts, our words, our attitudes, our motives, as well as our deeds and actions to Him and to the authority of His Word. Ask God to show where you are being conformed to the world's way of thinking and the world's way of doing things that are contrary to His ways. Sincerely, by faith, tell the Lord that you want Him to transform your life into the image of Christ and that you are ready to get serious about choosing right thoughts. Renewing your mind means adjusting your moral and spiritual vision and thinking to the mind of God that will have a transforming effect on your life. In other words, make it a habit to adjust your thinking to God's way of thinking. Choose to exchange your old natural, carnal, fleshly thoughts for God's higher thoughts.

Let's look at some examples to help you start the process of beginning to renew your mind.

The World's Way of Thinking	*God's Thinking*
"It's impossible"	"All things are possible with Me." (Luke 18:27)
"I'm too tired."	"I will give you rest." (Matthew 11:28–30)
"Nobody really loves me."	"I love you." (John 3:16)
"Nobody really cares for me."	"I care for you." (1 Peter 5:7)
"I can't go on."	"My grace is sufficient." (2 Corinthians 12:9)
"I can't figure things out."	"I will direct your steps." (Proverbs 20:24)
"I can't do this."	"You can do all things through Christ." (Philippians 4:13)
"I can't afford to…"	"I will supply all of your needs." (Philippians 4:19)

Power Meditation

> "Eye has not seen, nor ear heard, Nor have entered into the heart of man the things which God has prepared for those who love him" (1 Corinthians 2:9–10).

Day 2: A Surrendered Mind

Power Verse: "I beseech you, therefore, brethren, by the mercies of God, that you present your bodies a living sacrifice, holy, acceptable to God, which is your reasonable service." (Romans 12:1)

We learned yesterday that a renewed mind is the necessary link to being transformed into the image of Christ and experiencing the power of supernatural thinking. Today, we will discover how a surrendered mind is the first step to having a renewed mind. As long as we are operating with our own plans, programs, and agendas, we will not be able to see what God has planned for us. By having self-centered and self-motivated plans, we thwart God's purposes and plans for our lives. A life submitted to God's rule and authority and to His plans and purposes will be empowered by Him to accomplish all that He wants to accomplish. The reason so many Christians lack purpose and meaning in their lives is because they are trying to do their own thing, in their own way, with their own resources—when they should be relying on God for direction and resources. This type of self-centered thinking will only lead to a life full of anxiety and confusion.

Believe me, I have been there, done that. Not only will this self-centered thinking shut down God's power in our lives, but, as I found, we will not find the transformation taking place. Freedom in Christ comes as we turn the ownership of our lives over to God.

If you're having a difficult time in your Christian walk, you need to submit to God's authority. The only way to do that is to have your mind renewed with God's character, personality, and attributes.

49

We can only trust God and surrender to Him as we spend time with Him and come to know Him through the study of His Word.

Today, let's look at what the Bible teaches about a surrendered life and why it is necessary to renew our minds.

1. Look up the words *surrender* and *submit*. Record the definitions.
2. According to Romans 12:2, what will a surrendered will and a renewed mind enable us to do?
3. What does 2 Timothy 2:15 tell us about the study of God's Word?
4. God renews our mind through the Word. Read 2 Timothy 3:16–17. List the ways the Word instructs us.
5. God has recorded His thoughts for us in the Bible. He wants us to evaluate everything in our lives from His perspective and viewpoint. This is part of the renewing process.
6. What does God say about His ways and His thoughts in Isaiah 55:8–9?
7. What does God caution us concerning our thinking in Proverbs 3:5?
8. Read John 15:4–5. Why is it important to abide in the Lord?
9. When you must make decisions in your life, do you pray and ask God for His guidance, or do you "do your own thing?"
10. Read James 4:13–16. Why does he call the plans made by these individuals arrogant, boastful, and evil?
11. From these verses, what do you think should guide us when we make plans for the future?
12. On Day 1, we learned that renewing our minds means to adjust our thinking to God's way of thinking. What adjustments are you going to make to your thinking based on the truths you learned today?

Power Challenge

God's ways are not our ways, and His thoughts are higher than our thoughts. Thank the Lord that He has given us His Word and sealed us with His Spirit, empowering us with the ability to think His thoughts. We can experience the power in thinking God's way through the renewing of our minds. I want to challenge you to make a decision to choose right thoughts. Choose to set your mind on the things above. Choose not to entertain self-centered and self-seeking thoughts. Surrender your thoughts completely to God and watch Him as He transforms your life into one of power and purpose.

Power Meditation

> "Now to Him who is able to do exceedingly abundantly above all that we ask or think, according to the power that works in us" (Ephesians 3:20).

Day 3: Beware of Worldly Mindedness

Power Verse: "Do not love the world or the things in the world. If anyone loves the world, the love of the Father is not in Him." (1 John 2:15)

On days 1 and 2, we looked at two key Scriptures to help us understand the mind-renewing process. Let's summarize Romans 12:1–2.

1. God's purpose and plan for our lives is for us to live surrendered to Him and to His will.
2. We must stop being conformed to the world's ways of thinking and the world's way of doing things.
3. We must continue in the process of being changed into the image of Christ.
4. A transformed life will be the result of continually choosing to exchange our old worldly, fleshly thoughts for God's higher thoughts.

According to 1 Corinthians 2:16, we have the mind of Christ. God's goal for our thought lives is that we learn to think with the mind of Christ. By choosing to think fleshly and carnal thoughts, we never experience a real transformation and will live a defeated life.

The key to a transformed life is in continuing to choose right thoughts. Continuing—that's the key. Without continuing to choose, Christians often feel that their lives have become one giant roller coaster ride. We may be faithful in our striving to continue for a short time and even begin to see some spiritual growth, only to find ourselves slipping back into a pattern of spiritual slothfulness due to undisciplined minds. As Christians, we should have an effect on the world—not let the world affect us. Let's look into God's Word today and examine how the world might be affecting our thinking.

1. In 1 John 2:15, God says not to love the world or the things of the world. Read 1 John 2:16. What three things are not of God?

2. He lists the lust of the flesh, the lust of the eyes, and pride of life. The lust of the eyes and flesh is a strong desire or passion for something evil that brings pleasure to self. These strong desires are rooted in pride. Strong's Concordance defines pride (as it is used in this verse) as self-confidence or being dependent on self.

3. According to James 4:4–6, how does God view us when we become friendly with the world?

4. I believe we must give serious attention to James 4:3, which says that we become spiritual adulteresses and God's enemy when we become friendly with the world. *Philia* is the Greek word for friendship. It means to have a fond affection for someone; in this case, it would mean to have a fond affection for the world. In our homework for day 1, you looked up several definitions. I think we need to examine this passage of Scripture in light of those word studies.

    God doesn't want us to have a fond affection for the world's ways, values, and principles. God does not want the Christian to be conformed, shaped, or molded by the world but be transformed out of it by the renewing of our minds, which is made possible by the indwelling of the

Holy Spirit and the Word of God. When we walk in the world's ways, we make ourselves enemies of God.

5. What is the world's way? Who does the world exalt?

6. The world's way is to exalt self. Pride says self can make it happen, self is on the throne. Worldliness is a mindset rooted in pride that elevates self—self-centeredness, self-sufficiency, self-reliance, self-seeking, and self-motivated. This preoccupation with self-exalts oneself above God and leads one completely into a worldly lifestyle. Remember Proverbs 23:7 says, "For as he thinks in his heart, so is he."

7. According to James 4:6, how does God want His children to live?

8. Being proud is opposite to being humble. In 1 Peter 5:5–6, what is the warning and the promise given in this passage?

9. God opposes the proud, but He gives grace to the humble. It is God who exalts us—not we ourselves. The proud person depends on self for all the answers and the solutions. In contrast, the humble person is dependent on God for everything. The humble person places his trust and finds total sufficiency in God and God alone.

10. Jesus is our example, not the world. According to Philippians 2:5–9, list the ways that we can let the mind of Christ rule in our thinking.

11. According to Philippians 2:5–9, what did God do for Jesus because of His humbleness and His obedience?

12. In what areas of your life are you allowing the world to influence your thinking and that God wants to change?

Power Challenge

Worldliness is not how we dress or how we wear our hair or even what kind of car we drive. Worldliness is a mindset and an attitude rooted in self-centered thinking. One way you can recognize your worldliness is to look at how much time you spend preoccupied with self. Prayerfully, ask God to show you any areas of pride in your life that keep you from really enjoying God's best for you. Examine your thinking for self-centeredness, self-dependency, or self-sufficiency. As Christians, we need to avoid self-righteousness, thinking that I am righteous because of what I do or don't do. Our righteousness is in Christ. Remember 1 John 1:9, "If we confess our sins, He is faithful and just to forgive us our sins and to cleanse us from unrighteousness." Confession brings cleansing to our souls and restores us back into right fellowship with our Heavenly Father.

Power Meditation

"For whatever is born of God overcomes the world. And this is the victory that has overcome the world—our faith. Who is he who overcomes the world but he who believes that Jesus is the Son of God?" (1 John 5:4–5)

Day 4: Putting On the Mind of Christ and Putting Off the Mind of the Flesh

Power Verse: "For 'Who has known the mind of the Lord that he may instruct Him?' But we have the mind of Christ." (1 Corinthians 2:16)

As we learn more about renewing our minds and having the mind of Christ, we need to understand that this renewal process involves a deliberate act of our will—to choose to put off the old negative thoughts as well as put on God's thoughts.

God doesn't automatically give us His mind when we become born again. We must put off our own fleshly and carnal thinking. This involves confessing and repenting of our old mindsets. If we ask, God will give us the power and ability to discern everything that happens to us from His point of view. As we begin to do this, we will learn to rise above the circumstances in our lives and live as overcomers as He desires. It requires constant discipline not to give into those old negative thought patterns that keep us defeated. Instead, we must choose to take those thoughts captive to the obedience of Christ.

1. According to Isaiah 40:31, what is the result for one who waits on the Lord?
2. What bird is our renewed strength compared to?
3. If you have an encyclopedia, read up on eagles. What characteristics do they have that would help us to understand the process of renewing the mind?
4. Interestingly, eagles lose their old feathers after each molting season, and their physical strength is completely renewed. The new strength gives them the power to soar above their enemies.

    It is the same way with the Christian. As we put off the old carnal, fleshly thoughts and put on God's way of thinking, we receive His supernatural strength to soar above our enemies—the devil, the flesh, and the world.
5. Look up a definition for the word *soar* and record your insights.
6. Read Ephesians 4:17–32. Paul talks about things Christians are to put on and things they need to put off. According to verses 17–19, how should we walk?
7. Read Ephesians 4:20–32. Lists the things we are to "put off."

Now, list the things we are to "put on."

8. The phrases *put on* and *put off* can be found in Strong's Concordance or Vines Bible Dictionary. *Put off* means to lay aside, to take off, to put away—much like stripping off your clothes. On the other hand, *put on* means to apply, such as putting on clothes. Applied to our Christian walk, we are to strip off any ungodly thoughts or desires that attack our minds, just as you would take off any clothing that is offensive and put on more suitable clothes. I have certain colors of clothes in my closet that are quite becoming on me and others that are not. I naturally want to wear those colors I think are the most becoming. In the same way for Christians, there are certain thoughts, words, deeds, and actions that aren't becoming to who we are in

Christ. Stop *wearing* them. Put them off and put on those thoughts, words, and actions that become you as a child of God. Clothe your mind with renewed thoughts!

9. According to Colossians 3:1–2, where are we to place our minds?

10. What are we instructed to *put off* and to *put on* in Colossians 3:8–16?

11. Colossians 3:16 says we are to let the Word of Christ dwell in us "richly and in all wisdom." In James 3:13–18, James contrasts two types of wisdom: wisdom that is earthly, sensual, and demonic, and wisdom that is from above where Christ is seated. Write out the characteristics of these two types of wisdom.

12. Are you clothing your mind with renewed thoughts? What thoughts and attitudes do you need to put on or put off?

Power Challenge

Study Psalm 103:1–5. Meditate on these verses. During your prayer time, pray the verses. Bless His Holy Name! Thank Him for all His benefits. He is the one who forgives all your iniquities. He has healed all your diseases. He is the One who has redeemed your life. He crowns your life with lovingkindness and tender mercies. He satisfies your mouth with good things and thus renews your youth like the eagle's. Meditate means to think about, to ponder, to give close attention to. As you meditate on the wonder of who God is and how wonderful He is to you, God's power will begin to transform you!

Power Meditation

"I will praise You, for I am fearfully and wonderfully made; marvelous are Your works and that my soul knows very well" (Psalm 139:14).

Day 5: Quit Deceiving Yourself

Power Verse: "But be doers of the Word, and not hearers only, deceiving yourselves." (James 1: 22)

When I was first saved, I was so hungry for God's Word that I joined a Bible study class right away. A good friend recommended a Precept Bible study, so I signed up to do 1 John. Bible study became a very important part of my life. For several years of my Christian experience, I stumbled more than I walked. I was quite frustrated all the time because I wasn't seeing the spiritual growth that I thought I should be seeing.

My feelings and emotions were more in control of my life than the Holy Spirit. I was like the man James describes as being like a wave of the sea driven and tossed by the wind—up and down, up and down. My life was like a spiritual roller coaster ride. When I would share with other Christian friends the problems I was having, they would simply respond by saying, "Just pray more, or just get into the Word more, and everything will be okay."

Well, it wasn't okay. I was always involved in Bible studies, and as soon as I finished one, I would sign up for another. Out of desperation one day, I cried out to God in my prayers and told Him that I couldn't understand why I was continually having the same old sin problems. "Lord," I cried, "I've taken Bible study after Bible study for the last eight years. How many more Precept classes can I possibly take? I'm just a hopeless case!"

I thought Bible studies were supposed to be the answer. God, in His goodness and faithfulness, took me to James 1:22 and spoke clearly to my heart that I was a hearer of the Word and not a doer of the Word and that I was deceiving myself, believing that knowledge about the Bible was all it took to be victorious. When I finally realized that application of what I had been learning wasn't taking place in the way God intended, I then understood why there wasn't any transformation taking place and why my life was void of fruit. This truth totally revolutionized my Christian walk. I started getting victory in my life as I began to apply and practice principles from God's Word.

Sometimes, we think that as long as we are keeping the Ten Commandments, the "biggies," we are all right. In fact, God is just as interested in all those sins we have been considering as lesser sins in our minds. How about you? Are you daily applying and practicing God's Word to every situation of life, or are you deceiving yourself by believing that you are spiritual because you listen to a sermon every Sunday? Let's examine our lives today in light of what the Word of God says.

1. We have a responsibility to receive the Word and to practice the Word. Read James 1:19–25. According to verses 19 and 21, list the ways we are to receive the Word.

2. Verse 19 says we are to receive the implanted Word with meekness. Look up the definition of *meekness*, and in your own words, write your insight on how to receive God's word with meekness.

3. Are you receiving God's Word without struggling, fighting, or contending with God?

4. According to verse 19, what is the implanted Word able to do?

   When the Word of God becomes implanted, or rooted deeply, in our hearts and minds, it is able to save our souls. This doesn't mean that this is how we are saved. The word *save* in this passage means that the Word is able to protect and deliver us because it gives us wisdom and instruction as we live out our lives upon this earth.

5. In Matthew 13, Jesus gives the parable of the sower. He compares God's Word to seed and the human heart to soil. Read Matthew 13:3–8 and 18–23. Describe the four kinds of hearts that Jesus mentions in this parable.

6. What is the result of the life that receives, hears, and understands the Word, according to verse 23?

7. The Word of God cannot work in our lives unless we receive it in the right way. Jesus said in Matthew 13:13, "Hearing, they do not hear, nor do they understand." I believe many Christians are in this condition. They attend Bible studies and hear messages but are not experiencing spiritual

growth or bearing fruit. We must obey James's instructions on how to receive the Word.

A. Quick to Hear (James 1:19)—James exhorts us to be quick to hear. Jesus exhorted His followers in Matthew 13:9 by saying, "He who has ears to hear, let him hear!" We must guard against becoming dull of hearing when it comes to the hearing of God's Word. We can hear many sounds with our human ears, but there is a deeper kind of hearing that results in spiritual understanding. In Matthew 13:14, Jesus quoted from the prophecy of Isaiah, "Hearing, you will hear and shall not understand, and seeing, you will see and not perceive."

He is referring to hearing amiss, hearing without taking heed to what you have heard or neglecting what you have heard. Is your spiritual hearing dull or sharp?

B. Slow to Speak (James 1:19)—We have two ears and one mouth, which should remind us to listen more and speak less. When we talk too much and listen too little, we communicate to God that we think our own ideas are more important than His. James wisely advises us to reverse that process. Read Proverbs 10:19 and Proverbs 17:27 and record what these verses tell us about our words.

C. Slow to Anger or Wrath (James 1:19)—Do not get angry with God or His Word. James warns against anger that erupts when we think our opinions aren't being heard. Anger is the opposite of patience, the fruit that God wants to produce in our lives as we mature in Christ. Read Proverbs 14:29. What does this verse say about being slow to wrath?

D. A Prepared Heart (James 1:21)—James saw the human heart as a garden which, if left to itself, would produce only weeds. He exhorts us to pull up the weeds and prepare the soil of our hearts to receive the implanted Word. To prepare our hearts, we need to confess our sins and ask God for forgiveness. Then we need to thank Him for His grace, mercy, and forgiveness. Pray and ask God to plow up any hardness in your heart.

8. Read James 1:22–25. According to verse 22, what does James exhort us to do and what warning does he give?
9. In verses 23 and 24, what does James say about the person who is a hearer only?
10. Why do you and I use a mirror every day?
11. What spiritual flaws has God's Word shown you that need correcting in your life?
12. The last thing that James instructs us to do is be doers of the Word.

Practice the Word (James 1:22–25)—It is important to listen and hear the Word, but it is more important to obey what it says to do. That is being a doer of the Word. It is simple obedience to put into practice what you have heard and are learning. For many years, I had the mistaken idea that hearing a good sermon or doing a Bible study would somehow transform my life. It is not the hearing but the doing that brings God's blessings into our lives. We can read a chapter of the Bible every day, only to have it become a religious exercise and not benefit our lives. If we are to use God's mirror profitably, we must gaze into it carefully and with serious intent to put into practice what it says to do.

As we continue doing what James instructs us to do, we will experience transformation in our lives. The renewing of our minds comes as we allow God to change our thinking and as we become doers of His Word. God promises to bless us in what we do. Jesus said to His disciples in John 13:17, "If you know these things, [blessed] are you if you do them."

13. Are you a hearer or a doer of the Word?

Power Challenge

How did God speak to you today? Ask God to shine the search light of His Holy Spirit on your heart and to show you if you are a doer of His Word or a forgetful hearer. Maybe you started out with God on your spiritual journey, hearing, receiving, and practicing the Word, and after a time, you became cold and indifferent. Hebrews 5:11 calls this becoming "dull of hearing." Having God show us the truth about ourselves is not always a pleasant experience. God never shows us our weaknesses and mistakes just to cause pain. He wants us to confess our sins and mistakes to Him so that He can forgive and cleanse us and to ultimately bring about restoration in every area of our lives. Ask God to give you a soft and pliable heart that He can mold and shape into the image of His Son. That, my friend, is God's ultimate purpose for your life and mine—to transform us into the image of Jesus Christ. The world will be drawn to Jesus because they see Him in us, and then we will be able to make a difference in the world.

Power Meditation

"'O house of Israel, can I not do with you as this potter?' says the Lord. 'Look, as the clay is in the potter's hand, so are you in My hand, O house of Israel.'" (Jeremiah 18:6)

This verse is for you, beloved sister in Christ. Personalize this verse by putting your name in place of "O house of Israel" at the beginning and at the end.

Chapter 4
Practicing the Truth of Who I Am in Christ

Day 1: God's Grace

Power Verse: "But He was wounded for our transgressions, He was bruised for our iniquities; the chastisement for our peace was upon Him, and by His stripes we are healed." (Isaiah 53: 5)

As Christians, we need to walk in the truth of how much we are loved by God. I am awed by this passage of Scripture in Isaiah 53 because it shows me just how much God loves us. We must be very special to God for Him to allow Jesus to go to the cross and be crucified for our sins.

Just imagine what pain and agony Jesus felt as He carried that cross to Calvary. Isaiah 53:3 says Jesus was despised and rejected by men. He was "a man of sorrows and acquainted with grief…" Hebrews 12:2 says that Jesus "for the joy that was set before Him endured the cross, despising the shame, and has sat down at the right hand of the throne of God."

Jesus, who was the God Man—fully God and fully man—suffered more than anyone has ever suffered. He saw beyond the cross and was able to have joy because He knew that He was paying our sin debt in full. Colossians 2:14 says that at Calvary, Jesus "wiped out the handwriting of requirements that was against us… He has taken it out of the way, having nailed it to the cross." Jesus paid a debt that He did not owe. It was our debt—a debt we could not pay.

It is vitally important that Christians walk in the truth of who we are in Christ. We must know that God loves us with an uncon-

ditional, everlasting love. The world doesn't understand unconditional love. The world says we must perform well to earn approval.
Christians often find themselves caught in that performance trap.
We try to gain approval and self-worth through the acceptance of
others only to find ourselves unfulfilled. This search for self-worth
and significance often carries over into our relationship with God.
Mistakenly, we think that if we perform well; God will approve and
accept us. We are trying to earn God's love. We even erect strongholds of the mind that tell us we must perform to gain God's love
and approval.

God wants to free us from living under this bondage. You and
I can do nothing to make God love us more than He already does.
It's not about us and what we can do. It's about God's grace—pure
and simple.

We are saved by God's grace and kept by God's grace. Grace is
God's undeserved favor. Spelled out, GRACE is:

God's redemption at Christ's expense.

The performance trap will only lead us to serve God out of
duty. He wants us to serve Him out of delight. If you are captive to
the performance trap, somewhere along the way, your thinking has
become distorted about God and His love for you.

This week, we will examine God's Word to develop a better
understanding of who we are in Christ, our position in Christ, and
how we can experience freedom as we run the Christian race of faith.

There is no greater theme throughout Scripture than the rec-
onciliation of man to God. Today, we will look at Scriptures to see
how God has dealt with our sin and given us His promises of eternal
security.

1. Record any insecurities you feel regarding your relationship with your Heavenly Father. Do you have any areas in
   which you are trying to earn His love and approval?
2. According to John 3:16, what is God's promise to those
   who believe?
3. In John 5:24, what three things does Jesus promise to
   believers?

4. Jesus is our Great Shepherd, and we are His sheep. What does Jesus promise to His sheep in John 10: 27–29?
5. We have been justified through the blood of Jesus. Justified means "just as if I had never sinned." Read Romans 3:23–26. What do these verses teach about sin and redemption?

How much does our justification cost according to verse 24?

6. According to Romans 4:4–7, can we do anything to earn our righteousness?

Who is blessed according to verse 8?

7. Read 2 Corinthians 5:21. What do we learn about Jesus and our righteousness?
8. Read Romans 8:15–17. How does Paul describe our relationship with God?
9. Of what is Paul convinced in Romans 8:38–39?
10. According to 1 Peter 1:3–5, what assurances do we have concerning our salvation?
11. According to Psalm 103:12, what does God do with our sins?
12. Record the ways that God has spoken to you today.

What truths will you put into practice today?

Power Challenge

Do you really feel loved by God? Romans 4:8 says, "Blessed is the man to whom the Lord shall not impute sin." Do you feel *blessed*? You may be looking at your circumstances and present conditions and saying, "I don't feel very blessed." Well, beloved, if you are a born-again child of God, you are *blessed*. Based on what we studied today, let me tell you why you should rejoice. Because you are *blessed*! As a redeemed child of God, you have everlasting life, and no one can ever snatch you out of the Father's hands. You have been freely justified by God's grace through Christ. You have been declared righteous before God because Jesus is your righteousness. You have been adopted by God, and you are His heir and a joint heir with Christ, and nothing can ever separate you from the love of God. While on this earth, you are kept by His power and grace. You have an inheritance reserved and kept for you in heaven. God has removed your sin from Him as far as the east is from the west. Rejoice and stop trying to perform!

Power Meditation

> "The steps of a good man are ordered by the Lord, and He delights in his way. Though he falls, he shall not be utterly cast down; for the Lord upholds him with His hand" (Psalm 37:23–24).

Day 2: I Am a New Creation in Christ

Power Verse: "Therefore, if anyone is in Christ, he is a new creation; old things have passed away; behold, all things have become new." (2 Corinthians 5:17)

When we are born again and are in right standing with God, we are still tilted toward the world's way of thinking. Because we have been conditioned by the world's values and perspective, we find it difficult at times to break away. Many Christians are still trying to obtain significance by the world's way—by earning success and approval. We may find ourselves looking to other believers for answers when we should be going straight to Christ. This doesn't mean that we don't need each other. God uses other believers in our lives to demonstrate His love and acceptance toward us. He uses others to love, comfort, and encourage us. Just remember, whether or not we find acceptance in others, we need to know that Christ alone is the final authority when it comes to our worth and acceptance. We can be encouraged today because we are deeply loved by our Heavenly Father. We know we are completely forgiven, fully pleasing, totally accepted and complete in Christ.

Look up the following verses, which discuss who we are in Christ. In your own words, write down what each verse tells you about your new life in Him.

1. Romans 8:1–2

    Condemnation is from the devil. When the enemy brings you under guilt and condemnation, reject it in Jesus's name. Stand on Romans 8:1. The Holy Spirit convicts us of sin so that we might confess it to God and be cleansed and restored to a right relationship with Him. The devil wants to oppress us with thoughts of condemnation so as to keep us from enjoying our relationship with God. Revelation 12:10 says that the devil is the accuser of the brethren, and he goes before the throne of God, day and night to make accusations against us. Don't let the devil defeat you with condemnation!

2. Romans 8:37

3. What attitudes, mindsets, or actions do you need to ask Jesus to conquer in your life?

4. Read the following verses and describe your new position in Christ

    *   2 Corinthians 5:17
    *   Galatians 2:20–21
    *   Ephesians 1:7
    *   Ephesians 1:11–13
    *   Ephesians 2:1–10
    *   Colossians 2:10–13
    *   2 Timothy 1:8–9

5. 12 1 Peter 2:9–10

6. Let's review. As believers, our position in Christ is:

    *   In Christ, I have no condemnation.
    *   In Christ, I am more than a conqueror.
    *   In Christ, I am a new creation.

- In Christ, my trespasses have been forgiven.
- In Christ, I have been crucified. It is no longer I who live but Christ in me.
- In Christ, I have been redeemed and my sins forgiven.
- In Christ, I have obtained an inheritance.
- In Christ, I have been sealed with the Holy Spirit until the day of redemption.
- In Christ, I am His workmanship, created unto good works.
- In Christ, I am complete.
- In Christ, I am saved.
- In Christ, I have been called with a holy calling.
- In Christ, I am chosen. I am one of God's special people. I have obtained God's mercy.
- In Christ, I have been called out of darkness into His marvelous light.

7. Knowing this, list ways that you will want to change your attitude and outlook on life.
8. How has God spoken to you today?

Power Challenge

Pray and thank God for how wonderful He is for saving you and calling you out of darkness into His marvelous light. Jesus has given us so much to be grateful and thankful for. Ask God to help you develop an attitude of gratitude. It is an awesome privilege that we have been given to know God and to be able to call Him, Father. Romans 8:15 says that we have been adopted by God and that we call Him, "Abba Father," which is translated "Daddy." Go to your Heavenly Dad and tell Him how much you love Him. When discouragement and disappointments come, choose to meditate on who you are in Christ. Keep your eyes on Jesus, and the things of this world will grow strangely dim!

Power Meditation

> "Rejoice always, pray without ceasing, in everything give thanks; for this is the will of God in Christ Jesus for you" (1 Thessalonians 5:16–18).

Day 3: Jesus, "The Author and Finisher of Our Faith"

Power Verse: "Let us run with endurance the race that is set before us, looking unto Jesus, the Author and Finisher of our faith." (Hebrews 12:1–2)

The more we understand our position in Jesus Christ and the redemption He purchased for us, the greater our desire should be to please God and to obey Him. God's desire for His children is that we keep moving forward, that we run the race and fight the good fight of faith. In Hebrews 6:1, the writer exhorts us to press on to maturity. In Hebrews 12:1–2, our Power Verse for today, the writer compares the Christian life to running a race, and we are told to run with endurance. How do we run with endurance? Life is tough at best. We all experience trials and adversities and endure much suffering along the way. You may have felt, at one time or another, that you could not endure any longer and wanted to give up. It isn't necessary for any believer to give up or to go backward. Hebrews 12:1–3 gives us a number of ways to stay encouraged and to run the race successfully.

On days 4 and 5, we will examine Hebrews 12:1–3, as well as other Scriptures, to get a better understanding of the Christian race, how we can be encouraged and experience God's freedom as we run our race of endurance.

The Runner

> "Do you not know that those who run in a race all run, but one receives the prize? Run in such a way that you may obtain it." (1 Corinthians 9:24)

1. Read Hebrews 12:1–2. List everything that as runners we need to do.

2. List the attitudes and disciplines we need as we run the race according to 1 Corinthians 9:24–27.

3. According to Hebrews 12:2, who are we to focus on as we run the race?

4. Who is Jesus in relationship to our faith?

   Depending on what Bible translation you are using, the words used in this passage may be *looking unto Jesus, fixing our eyes,* or *setting our eyes upon Jesus, the Author and Finisher of our faith.* To look means to use the power of sight to see, to direct our gaze or attention to, to face or aim in a certain direction. To set means to fix, put, or place in a firm and secure position. As we run this race, we are to choose to direct our attention and fix firmly our focus and aim upon Jesus because our position in the race is secure in Him. We don't want to run our race aimlessly as 1 Corinthians 9:26 warns against. Rather, we want to run in such a way that we will obtain the prize. We want to run with a winning attitude.

5. Hebrews 12:1–2 says to "lay aside every weight and the sin which so easily ensnares us, and let us run with endurance the race that is set before us, looking unto Jesus, the Author and Finisher of our faith."

   Look up the definitions of these words and record your insights:

   In a physical sense, what does running a race involve? It means training and getting into shape. You must get your body lean so that you will not run with a lot of extra weight. You wouldn't run a 100-yard dash carrying a 50-pound sack of potatoes, would you? The same is true as we run our Christian race. We need to lay aside those hindrances that keep us from running the race successfully. Sin is missing the mark. It is running independently of God. While not necessarily bad things, hindrances are things that distract us and divide our attention. Hindrances keep us from focusing on God and keep us from progressing in our spiritual lives. Hindrances prevent us from enjoying the power of supernatural thinking because they keep our minds distracted and divided. The devil loves to keep us distracted because we then often become confused and miss God's purpose and plan for our lives.

The Lord showed me a few years ago, when I was struggling so much with my thought life, that I had allowed my daughter, Keri, to become a hindrance. While she was (and still is) one of the greatest blessings in my life, I had also let her become an encumbrance. So much of my thought-life revolved around her that I found myself worrying about her all the time. As a matter of fact, I would consider my thinking at that time on the compulsive and obsessive side! Finally, when she left home to go to college, God brought me to my knees and to an altar experience where He required me to release Keri completely to Him. What a freeing experience that was! My mind was actually freed up to begin focusing on my life and what God wanted me to do. I urge you to seriously examine your life for hindrances.

Power Challenge

In the light of what you have learned today, examine your life for sins and hindrances—anything that would hinder you from moving forward in your Christian life. List them on a sheet of paper. Then release each one to God and ask Him to give you the courage, strength, and power to lay them aside so that you can run the race with endurance. Prayerfully, ask Him to order your thoughts and to help you keep your focus on Jesus, the Author and Finisher of your faith.

Power Meditation

"Holding fast the word of life, so that I may rejoice in the day of Christ that I have not run in vain or labored in vain" (Philippians 2:16).

Day 4: The Race

Power Verse: "And everyone who competes for the prize is temperate in all things. Now they do it to obtain a perishable crown, but we for an imperishable crown." (1 Corinthians 9:25)

Yesterday, we saw that the Christian life is like running a race. The Christian race begins the day we are saved and ends the day we meet Jesus face-to-face. If we are going to successfully run the race to the finish and win the prize, we need to put aside sin and hindrances in our lives. Sin and hindrances trip us up and make us stumble and fall before we reach the goal. I believe the sin that the writer of Hebrews speaks of is the sin of unbelief because the emphasis of his writings is on faith. Unbelief was the sin that kept the children of Israel from going in and possessing the Promised Land. Faith moves us forward and unbelief moves us backward. Faith comes as we look toward Christ, trusting and relying on Him. Jesus is not only standing at the finish line to welcome us into heaven, but He is also standing beside us to guide, strengthen, and encourage us as we run the race of faith.

1. Read Hebrews 12:1–3. According to verse 1, what race are we to run?

    God has a plan and purpose for our lives. He has assigned a lane for each of us to run in and has equipped us to run. We should never run someone else's race—only the one that has been set before us. If our race seems difficult, disappointing, or demanding, it could be that we have left our assigned lane and are trying to run someone else's race.

2. How does Psalm 37:23–24 describe the race before us?

3. According to Proverbs 20:24, who directs our race?

    Do we need to understand everything that is happening in our lives in order to run the race of life?

4. According to Proverbs 3:5–6, what should our thinking and attitude be as we run our race of faith?

What does God promise us?

5. Read James 1:2. What should we expect to encounter on our race?

6. James tells us that trials test our faith. According to James 1:3–4, what qualities does God want to produce in our lives as a result of trials?

7. Look up the definitions for the following words and record your insights:

Trials
Endurance, patience or perseverance
Perfect or mature
Complete

8. According to 1 Peter 4:12, how should we think about trials?

9. According to 1 Peter 4:13, what should our attitude be concerning trials?

10. What should our attitude be concerning trials according to James 1:2?

11. How would you describe your attitude and thinking when you go through various trials?

Power Challenge

When James says to count it all joy when you encounter trials, he is not saying that your trial is going to be joyful, but rather, our attitude toward the trial should be joyful. "To count" is a financial term. It means to evaluate. When we face trials, we must evaluate them in the light of what God is doing in us. Our values will determine how we evaluate trials. If we value comfort more than character, then trials will upset us and make us bitter. If we value temporal things more than eternal things, then we will not be able to count it all joy when trials come our way. God desires that trials make us better Christians and not bitter Christians.

Trials come in all shapes and sizes. They usually come into our lives unexpectedly. Some trials are divinely permitted and sent into our lives by God for the purpose of perfecting and maturing us. Everything that God allows to come into our lives has first been sifted through His hands of love. God never desires for trials to hurt or to harm us but to develop strong Christian character in us.

Power Meditation

"We also glory in tribulations, knowing that tribulation produces perseverance" (Romans 5:3).

Day 5: Our Reward for Running the Race with Endurance

Power Verse: "Therefore, do not cast away your confidence, which has great reward. For you have need of endurance, so that after you have done the will of God, you may receive the promise." (Hebrews 10:35–36)

We are told by God that we need endurance. Endure is not a word that is very popular today among Christians. Our thinking has been reduced to a microwave mentality. When hard times come upon us, our tendency is to try and figure out how we are going to handle it and what is the quickest way out. Prayer is usually the last thing we do. And if we don't get answers in record speed, we start worrying and fretting about our situation instead of trusting and leaning on the Lord. Endurance is the capacity to withstand pressure. The Greek word is *hupomone*, which means to bear up under the pressure of something. Endurance involves patience. It is a courageous abiding and waiting while suffering hardships and affliction. The question we need to ask ourselves is, How are we enduring?

When trials come—and they will come—do you shift into a self-sufficient mindset that says, "I will get through this one way or another!" Or perhaps you handle trials with a "grin and bear it" attitude, only to find yourself tied up in knots, wringing your hands, pacing the floor all day, and losing sleep at night. When trials come, we will do one of two things. We will either handle the trial God's way, or we will handle the trial our way.

To develop endurance while going through a trial, Christians must keep focused on the Burden-Bearer and not the burden. We will crater if we try to carry the burdens of life in our own strength. We are able to bear up under the pressure because we are drawing our strength from God, who gives us the ability to endure through the power of the Holy Spirit.

Don't fall into the trap by thinking you must find your own way when dealing with hardships. Stand on the Word of God. That is the only way.

1. Read 1 Corinthians 10:13. How can meditating on this verse give you comfort in the midst of trials?
2. Who provides the way of escape in trials?
3. Read Daniel chapter 3. This chapter gives the account of how Nebuchadnezzar had Shadrach, Meshach, and Abednego thrown into the fiery furnace because they would not bow down and worship the golden image. According to verses 17–19, what was their response to the king's demand?
4. According to Daniel 3:24–27, what was God's way of escape for the three Hebrew men? Were they delivered from the trial or in the midst of the trial?
5. Sometimes, God delivers us from trials, but most of the time, He brings deliverance in the midst of our trial, just as He did for Shadrach, Meshach, and Abednego. Think about your own life. Write down times when God has delivered you in the middle of difficult circumstances by giving you supernatural peace and strength to endure the storm.
6. Read Isaiah 43:1–2. List all the promises that comfort us during storms of life.
7. Have you experienced times of suffering when you felt like God had forgotten you? Read Psalm 139:1–4. How well is God acquainted with your circumstances?

It is so important to remember when we are going through trials that God is in control of our lives and our circumstances. He is a Sovereign, All-powerful, All-knowing, and Mighty God. He has promised to never leave us nor forsake us. He is trustworthy and faithful and will not allow us to suffer beyond what we are able to bear but will provide a way of escape.

8. In James 1:12, how does James describe the man who endures trials?

9. Look up a definition for the word *blessed* and record your insights.

10. According to 2 Timothy 2:1–5, how should we handle hardships? What should our relationship be with this world and Christ?

11. What does God desire to do in our lives through suffering, according to 1 Peter 5:10?

12. According to Romans 5:1–5, what spiritual aspects will be produced as a result of tribulation?

13. What does the Holy Spirit do in our times of waiting, hoping, and persevering, according to Romans 8:24–28?

14. According to Hebrews 217, what is Jesus doing for us as we run our race with endurance?

15. How are you enduring the trials of life? Are they making you bitter or better?

As children of God, we can be encouraged as we endure trials and adversities because we are not going through them alone. We have the indwelling presence and power of the Holy Spirit. He not only gives us the power to endure, but He also prays for us when we don't know how to pray. He intercedes for us according to the will of God. Jesus's present day ministry is a ministry of intercession. We can endure because Jesus is interceding for us. Hebrews 2:17–18 says that Jesus had to be made like His brethren, that He might be a merciful and faithful High Priest. Because He Himself suffered and was tempted, He is able to aid those who are tempted. We will be rewarded for enduring trials.

Rewards of Character and Crowns

Endurance develops Christian character in this life, which glorifies God. And if we endure trials, we will receive the Crown of Life when Jesus returns. There are five crowns mentioned in the Scriptures to be given to believers on the basis of merit. They are the Crown of Rejoicing (1 Thessalonians 2:19 and Philippians 4:1), Incorruptible Crown (1 Corinthians 9:24–27), Crown of Righteousness (2 Timothy 4:7–8), Crown of Life (James 1:12), and the Crown of Glory (1 Peter 5:1–4). I encourage you to study these Scriptures describing crowns that will be given to believers at the Judgment Seat of Christ.

Power Challenge

What does God want to change in your thinking as a result of what you have studied this week? Pray and ask God to help you to practice the truth of who you are in Christ and to enable you to experience His love as never before. Examine your life for attitudes and thinking that could be hindering your spiritual progress. It could be the hindrance of being caught in a performance trap, self-sufficiency, or an inability to trust God in times of distress. Perhaps, you have been trying to carry burdens that God never intended for you to carry. God's Word says in 1 Peter 5:7 that we are to cast our cares upon Jesus because He cares for us. Jesus loves you, and He wants to be your Burden Bearer. Thank Him for the character that He is building in you through every circumstance of life and for the Crown of Life that awaits you in glory.

Power Meditation

"And we know that all things work together for good to those who love God, to those who are the called according to His purpose" (Romans 8:28).

Chapter 5
Exposing Stinking Thinking

Day 1: Laying Aside Bitterness

Power Verse: "Not what goes into the mouth defiles a man; but what comes out of the mouth, this defiles a man." (Matthew 15:11)

Thoughts are unspoken words. When our thoughts become words, they expose the true condition of our hearts. Jesus said in Matthew 12:34 that "out of the abundance of the heart, the mouth speaks." To identify the "stinking thinking" in our lives, all we have to do is listen to our words. Do you talk differently at home than you do at church? What do you say when someone pulls out in front of your car and immediately puts on their brakes? How do you communicate with your spouse or your children when you are in the midst of difficult circumstances? What words do you speak to your best friend when someone has behaved rudely to you, hurting your feelings?

This week, we will examine our lives for bitterness, strife, envy, anger, and judging—all negative mindsets and forms of stinking thinking that can become strongholds in our lives. They need to be exposed, dealt with, and given up because they are poisonous toxins to our soul that will cripple our spirits and keep us from running our Christian race with freedom and endurance. Stinking thinking leads to words that are foul and offensive, not only to God and others but to ourselves as well. Stinking thinking is a hindrance to the Christian life that, if not dealt with, will hinder our spiritual progress. The Scriptures we will study are written to our brothers and sisters in Christ. God's desire is for the church to walk in unity. When we see bitterness, envy, and strife among the brethren, there is no unity, peace, or love in the church—and that destroys our witness for the Lord to the lost world.

1. Look up the word *defile* and record its meaning.
2. According to Jesus in Matthew 15:10–11, 17–20, where does defilement flow from?
3. List the actions and sins that come forth from the heart in Matthew 15:19.
4. Can you recall words that you have spoken and later regretted? Did you wonder where the words came from?
5. Look up the word *bitterness* and record your insights.
6. What does Hebrews 12:15 say that a root of bitterness will do in our lives?
7. Where does Jesus say bitterness flows from in Mathew 15:19?
   Roots of bitterness are roots that have grown deep and have become firmly established. The author of Hebrews is speaking about bitterness that has put down roots. It dwells within us and disrupts at will. *Pikra* is the Greek word for bitterness. It means to cut, to prick, pointed, sharp, a pungent taste, or smell. Just imagine walking outside with your bare feet and stepping on a tack. Ouch! That sharp, cutting pain is what it is like to live with bitterness in our lives.
8. Roots of bitterness may remain dormant for a while, only to surface again, pricking our thoughts with painful memories. In your life, what painful experiences continue to carry the sting of bitterness?
9. Bitterness is an angry, resentful state of mind that can especially be seen when we are going through trials and adversities. The experiences that God intends for our good can be twisted into bitterness. The Lord says in Hebrews 12 that whom He loves, He chastens. Chasten means to discipline and to train, and it is used with the idea of child training. God is training us as His children to trust and obey Him and to develop Christ-likeness in our lives. As we have seen in a prior chapter, His goal is to use all our life circumstances to make us better—not bitter. According

to Hebrews 12:5–11, how are we to view the chastening of the Lord? What is God's desired outcome for chastening, according to verses 10–11?

10. Does Hebrews 12:14–15 tell us why are we to seek peace and holiness?

11. In context with what you have studied about God's discipline, according to Hebrews 12:15, why do you think we are warned against bitterness?

12. Bitterness has a way of spreading and corrupting and polluting the minds of others. We can speak words that build up and edify others, or we can speak words that tear them down. Jesus said that we are defiled by the words of our mouth. If we speak bitter, angry, and resentful words, it is because we have first had bitter, angry, and resentful thoughts. Read Matthew 12:34. What do you think Jesus was trying to teach us about our thought lives?

13. Whether we are dealing with bitterness as a result of betrayal, divorce, rejection, or having our reputations destroyed by lies, God's grace is the cure. God gives us the grace and ability to forgive those who have hurt and wronged us. According to Ephesians 4:30–32, what does Paul instruct us to do when dealing with bitterness and anger?

14. Forgiveness is a divine miracle and key to overcoming a bitter, angry mindset. You may be angry with yourself, angry with another person, angry over a situation, or even angry with God. Forgiveness means to let go, cancel, release, and pardon. What does Jesus's parable in Matthew 18:21–35 teach us about releasing others?

15. What are we exhorted to do in Colossians 3:12–13?

16. If we are to follow Jesus's example in Luke 23:32–34, how should we deal with bitterness and unforgiveness?

Power Challenge

Examine your life for bitterness and unforgiveness. Pray and ask God to show you if there are any past hurts and rejection from others that you buried and did not really deal with. Ask your Heavenly Father to reveal to you anyone to whom you have spoken harsh, bitter words for which you need to go and ask for forgiveness. Be willing to do whatever the Lord requires you to do. Jesus said in Matthew 18:35 that we would be turned over to the tormentors if we choose not to forgive our brothers and sisters of their trespasses. Bitterness and unforgiveness will torment our minds if we let them. I encourage you to make a choice today to lay aside the destructive mindset of bitterness and put on tender mercies, kindness, humility, meekness, and patience, bearing with one another and forgiving one another, just as Christ forgave you.

Power Meditation

> "Create in me a clean heart, O God,
> And renew a steadfast spirit within me.
> Do not cast me away from your presence,
> And do not take Your Holy Spirit from me.
> Restore to me the joy of Your salvation,
> And upload me with Your generous Spirit" (Psalm 51:10–12).

Day 2: Freedom from a Life of Strife

Power Verse: "Hatred stirs up strife, but love covers all sins." (Proverbs 10:12)

The world is looking for peace and can't find it. Jesus said to His followers in John 14:27, "Peace I leave with you...not as the world gives do I give to you. Let not your heart be troubled, neither let it be afraid." Not only is the world looking for peace, but the Church of Jesus Christ is looking for peace as well. How do we find the peace that Jesus describes in this verse? One of the greatest enemies to the Christian's peace is strife. Strife is quarreling, bickering, contentions, factions, discord and conflict. Strife is an angry undercurrent. Strife is a demonic spirit sent from Satan himself to destroy lives. Strife unattended will destroy marriages, relationships, businesses and ministries. When strife is present in our lives, it will destroy our happiness and our peace of mind. Just as peace is a fruit of the Spirit, strife is carnal and a fruit of the flesh. To have a life that is free from strife, we must choose to walk in love and to pursue peace at any price. That might mean holding our tongues. It might mean that we don't always have to be right. Perhaps it means that we will have to ask for forgiveness from our spouses, or children, or a friend. Today we will see what God's Word says about strife and how we can live free from a life of strife.

1. Read Genesis 13:1–11. How did Abraham deal with strife in his relationship with his nephew, Lot?
2. Think about your own life. Are you willing to separate yourself from your rights and give them up in order to keep peace between you and another person?
3. According to 1 Corinthians 3:1–4, how does Paul describe the Christian who is walking in strife?
4. How are we to deal with strife according to the following verses?

   Proverbs 17:14
   2 Timothy 2:22–26
   Titus 3:9–11

5. What were Pauls concerns & fear about the Corinthian church in 2 Corinthians 12:20–21?

In 2 Corinthians 13:11, what did he admonish them to do about the problem?

6. What is the source of strife and quarrels that James addresses in James 4:1?
7. What is the result of their fights and quarrels, as recorded in James 4:2–4?
   From what we have studied so far, we can see that strife is a spirit that causes fights, quarrels, factions, and contentions with others. There can be no peace when strife

is at work in our lives. We can't walk in love and walk in strife at the same time. Strife will keep us at war with God, others, and ourselves.

8. Do you have relationships that always seem to lead you into contentions, quarreling, or disputes? If so, how do you feel God is impressing you to deal with these relationships?
9. What are God's solutions to strife according to 1 Peter 3:8–12?
10. Look up the definition for the following words:
11. Sometimes, I think we are guilty of praying for peace yet not eliminating those things from our lives that cause strife and make us lose our peace. Peace is something that we must seek to achieve and accomplish. We must pursue peace with diligence. If I know that certain situations are going to lead me into strife and take my peace, I need to avoid them. If I know that certain conversations will lead me into strife, I need to avoid them. What types of thinking, actions, or situations do you need to avoid in order to eliminate strife and have peace?

Power Challenge

Read 1 Corinthians 13, the love chapter, and make a list of all the attributes of love. As you study this list, keep in mind that these are the attributes of God because we know that God is love. Prayerfully, ask God to show you areas in your own life in which you need to develop more of His attributes. Choose to lay aside strife in your life and walk in love and peace.

Power Meditation

"'God resists the proud but gives grace to the humble.' Therefore, humble yourselves under the mighty hand of God, That He may exalt you in due time" (1 Peter 5:5–6).

Day 3: Envy and Jealousy: The Twin Sins

Power Verse: "If you have bitter envy and self-seeking in your hearts, do not boast and lie against the truth. This wisdom does not descend from above but is earthly, sensual, demonic." (James 3:14–15)

We have dealt with the fact that the devil, the world, and the flesh are three enemies that attack every believer's thinking. We must carefully make decisions that are guided by God's wisdom. There is a heavenly wisdom that is from God above, and there is man-made wisdom, which is not from God but rather is earthly, sensual, and demonic. 1 Corinthians 2:14 says that man's wisdom is foolishness to God and that God's wisdom is foolishness to man. Man's wisdom comes from reason, and God's wisdom comes from revelation. Man's earthly wisdom will come to nothing, while God's wisdom will endure forever. God's wisdom operates differently from the wisdom that is earthly, sensual, and demonic. They originate from different sources, and they operate in opposite ways.

One of the evidences of false wisdom is found in thinking that is envious and jealous of others. Do we rejoice when others succeed? Or do we become envious and suspicious of that person? Do we feel burdened when others fail? Or are we secretly glad of their failure? When the wisdom of the world gets into the church, there is a great deal of fleshly promotion and human glorification going on. As children of God, we should never allow ourselves to become envious or jealous of others. Instead, God would have us to rejoice with others for their success and accomplishments. Envy and jealousy are destructive mindsets that hinder us in our Christian race.

Let's examine God's Word to learn more about envy and jealousy and practical ways to overcome these destructive mindsets.

1. Look up the definition for the following words.

    Envy
    Jealous or Jealousy

2. In 1 Samuel 17, we have the account of David killing the giant, Goliath, and winning the favor of King Saul. David goes to live in Saul's palace and becomes best friends with Saul's son, Jonathan. David was able to kill a giant, but he ended up living with a bigger giant, Saul, one he could not kill. We see in 1 Samuel 18 that Saul's attitude toward David drastically changes because Saul had become very envious and jealous of David's popularity. Read through 1 Samuel 18 and list all the types of thinking and behavior that jealousy and envy toward David produced in Saul's life.

3. According to 1 Samuel 18:5, 14, 30, what guided David's thinking and actions?

4. In studying Saul's life, we see that envy and jealousy are strong emotions that can lead into all types of irrational thinking and behavior. During every waking moment, Saul plotted and planned ways to destroy David. Describe the "Sauls" you have had to deal with in your own life.

5. Read James 3:17 and list the attributes of Godly wisdom.

6. According to James 3:14–16, describe what envy and self-seeking produce in our hearts.

   James says that when we walk in envy and jealousy toward others, we are not walking in God's wisdom. Instead, we are walking in a wisdom that is carnal, fleshly, and demonic. Envy and jealousy produce resentful, ill-willed, spiteful, and covetous thoughts toward another person, and they shut down the power of the Holy Spirit from working in our lives.

7. Paul admonished the Corinthian church in 1 Corinthians 3:3 by saying they were carnal and walking in the flesh because envy and strife was evident among them, causing divisions. According to Romans 8:5–8, what does walking in the flesh and being carnally minded produce in our lives?

8. What does Paul exhort us to do in order to overcome envy, strife, and jealousy in Romans 13:13–14?

9. Envy and jealousy are fruits of the flesh. If we want to combat and overcome envy and jealousy, we must walk in the

power of the Holy Spirit and allow God to produce the fruit of the Spirit in our lives. Read Galatians 5:22–23. List the fruits of the Spirit.

10. What warning are we given in Galatians 6:7–8, and what are we exhorted to do in verses 9–10?

11. Which fruits of the Spirit do you desire God to produce in your life?

Envy and jealousy can be seen in families, marriages, ministries, businesses, and friendships. When we are envious or jealous of another person, it is because we have been threatened by their success, popularity, accomplishments, or perhaps even their appearance. Women especially have this problem because we have bought into the lie that tells us we need to have a "number 10" body in order to feel good about ourselves. Capooy to that lie!

12. God resists the proud, but He gives grace to the humble. We cannot walk with envy and jealousy in our lives and, at the same time, walk humbly before the Lord. According to James 4:7–10, what steps do we need to take to overcome thoughts of envy and jealousy?

13. What does God promise to do if we humble ourselves before Him, according to James 4:10?

14. How has God spoken to you today?

Power Challenge

If you have identified areas of envy and jealousy in your life, take it to the Lord in prayer. Envy and jealousy are sin and hinder us from running our race successfully. First John 1:9 promises that if we will confess our sins to the Lord, He will be faithful and just to forgive us and cleanse us of all unrighteousness. Ask God to provoke within you a willingness to submit to Him, to draw near to Him, and to have a repentant heart. If you have been making choices to walk in the flesh instead of the Spirit, ask God to help you make right choices. Choose to walk by the Spirit, and you will not fulfill the lust of the flesh. Remember, God is the One who knows you best and the

One who loves you the most. Don't ever be afraid to confess sin to God. He already knows about it! Confession brings cleansing to our souls and restores us back into fellowship with our Heavenly Father.

Power Meditation

> "The sacrifices of God are a broken spirit, a broken and a contrite heart, these, O God, You will not despise" (Psalm 51:17).

Day 4: The Poison and Passion of Anger and Wrath
Power Verse: "Be angry, and do not sin, do not let the sun go down on your wrath." (Ephesians 4:26)

We are told to be angry, but do not sin. The rest of this verse tells us how. When we get angry, we are to deal with it and get over it quickly. Anger that is sinful is a habitual state of being angry. It is anger that we invite into our lives and entertain for long periods of time. This type of anger just keeps on growing because we feed and nurse it over and over. It is anger that we replay, rehearse, and rehash in our minds. Vines Dictionary defines anger in its Greek form as *orge*, used to describe the wrath of man. It is the strongest passion of all emotions and is a settled, abiding condition of the mind with a frequent view to punish or get revenge. The Greek word for wrath is *thumas*, which indicates a more agitated condition of the feelings, an outburst of wrath from inward indignation. Orge is less sudden in its rise than thumas but more lasting in nature. Thumas expresses more of the inward feeling and orge a more active emotion. Thumas is characterized by quickly blazing up and quickly subsiding. *Parorgismos* is Greek for anger and points to that which provokes to wrath and suggests a less continued state than orge. Synonyms for anger are provoke, wrath, rage, animosity, passion, fury, and hostility. Anger left unleashed and not under the control of the Holy Spirit can lead to self-destruction.

Today, we will look at what the Word of God teaches about anger and how we should handle anger in our own lives.

1. Read Genesis 4:1–6 about Cain and Abel. We want to look at anger in the life of Cain and where it led him.

2. According to verses 2–5, what caused Cain to become angry at Abel?

3. Cain resented the fact that God accepted Abel's offering and rejected his offering. He became angry. How does anger affect his appearance according to verse 5?

4. Have you ever been so angry that it was obvious by your facial expression? If so, describe that time.

5. How did God respond to Cain's anger in verses 6–7?

6. What resulted from Cain's uncontrolled anger, according to verse 8?

7. In verses 9–16, how did God punish Cain for killing Abel?

8. God told Cain in verse 7 that the sin of his anger wanted to rule him, but God said Cain was to rule over it. Cain could have chosen to repent of his anger and get right with God and with Abel. Instead, he chose not to, and anger got the best of him. Are you dealing with any negative circumstances in your life right now that are directly related to making a bad choice when you were angry?

9. As we have seen from Cain's life, anger is a very strong emotion—one that can lead to killing another person. Can you remember any time when you have had your spirit killed by the words spoken to you by an angry person or a time when you killed another's spirit with your angry words?

10. Read the following Scriptures, and write down what each one instructs us to do with anger and wrath. What are the solutions to overcoming anger?

    Ephesians 4:31 to 5:1–2
    Colossians 3:8, 12–15
    James 1: 19 - 21
    Proverbs 22:24–25
    Proverbs 25:23–24
    Proverbs 29:22–23

11. What do we learn from Jesus concerning anger, and what warning does He give us in Matthew 5:22?

12. Angry people are easily offended, easily provoked, critical, and super sensitive. Many times they can be mad at another person for no cause or reason. Do you ever have times when you're angry about something or someone and then, later, not even remember why you were angry in the first place?

13. Read Matthew 5:23–24. If we are angry or in strife with a brother, what does Jesus say we are to do concerning bringing our gifts to the altar?

    This is a very serious passage of Scripture. I don't believe Jesus is just talking about our tithe that we bring to church on Sunday but the gift of our praise, our worship, and our prayers. This Scripture clearly teaches us that if we don't get right with a brother with whom we are angry or in strife, God will not receive our tithe, our prayers, our worship, or our praise. I encourage you to seriously examine your life for any unresolved conflicts with another brother or sister in Christ. If you don't, your relationship with God will suffer.

    Anger and wrath are fruits of the flesh, and self-control is a fruit of the Spirit. If you are bothered with angry thoughts only occasionally or if you have a deep-seated type of anger, self-control is the fruit of the Spirit that can combat anger. God has given us self-control so we can discipline ourselves to make good choices in life. Self-control empowers us to be motivated, not by how we feel but what we choose to do. A person who has self-control exercises self-restraint in actions and in speech. Controlling our mouths can be tough. Proverbs 19:11 tells us that the discretion of a man makes him slow to anger, and his glory is to overlook a transgression. If I am acting wisely, I won't let myself become angry every time someone offends me. It is vital that Christians learn to exercise self-control and restraint. Matthew 12:33 says that a tree is known by its fruit, the same is true of our Christian lives.

14. God told Cain to rule over his passion of anger so that it would not rule over him. What does Proverbs 25:28 say about the man who has no rule or self-control in his life?

15. Without self-control, we are like a broken down city without walls. Webster's defines wall as a continuous defensive rampart, something that surrounds, separates, and protects. Based on this definition and Proverbs 25:28, explain in your own words what exercising self-control provides in our lives.

16. How powerful is the person who is slow to anger, according to Proverbs 16:32?

Making right choices in life is so important. In Deuteronomy 30:19, God says, "I have set before you, life and death, blessing and cursing, therefore choose life, that both you and your descendants may live." We must choose to not hold on to anger and choose to exercise self-control. We must choose to walk in the power of the Holy Spirit. Then we will make wise choices and reap the benefits of wisdom. Wisdom is having a deep understanding of the ways and purposes of God. If we walk in wisdom, we will walk free of anger and hostility and our paths will be straight.

Power Challenge

James says that we are to combat anger and wrath by receiving the implanted word with meekness, which is able to save our souls. To receive the word with meekness, we are to receive it with patience, gentleness, and submission. Have you been submitting to God's Word by being obedient to do what His Word says to do? God's Word is wisdom and counsel for life. It will protect us from making wrong choices when we heed it. The Word is our defensive weapon against Satan. Prayerfully, ask God to help you choose to be obedient to His Word. Ask Him to show you any areas of anger in your life. Ask yourself the following questions:

1. Am I easily offended?
2. Am I easily provoked?
3. Am I critical toward certain people?
4. Am I super sensitive?
5. Do I backbite other people when given the opportunity?

Confess any anger to God and ask Him to show you anyone from whom you need to ask forgiveness due to an angry spirit. God is always ready to forgive, heal, and restore us. He is simply waiting for us to ask Him. Remember, He is our Heavenly Dad, and He loves us with an unconditional love.

Power Meditation

"Have mercy upon me, O God,
according to Your lovingkindness;
according to the multitude of Your tender mercies,
blot out my transgressions.
Wash me thoroughly from my iniquity,
and cleanse me from my sin" (Psalm 51:1–2).

Day 5: Quit Judging and Criticizing
Power Verse: "Judge not, that you be not judged." (Matthew 7:1)

People do not enjoy being around others who are judgmental and critical. No one likes to be around people who constantly voice their opinion about everything. Vines Dictionary defines judgment as a decision passed on the faults of others and is cross-referenced to the word *condemnation*. One of the Greek words for judge means to form an opinion and is cross-referenced to the word *sentence*. God is the only One who has the authority to condemn or sentence. When we form an opinion and judge another person in a condemning way, we are setting ourselves up as God. Judgment and criticism are fruits of the root of pride. God hates the sin of pride. Pride caused Lucifer's fall as well as Adam and Eve's fall. When we judge and criticize others, we are sure to fall as well. Proverbs 16:18 says that pride goes before the fall. We will be looking at a lot of Scriptures today that will help us understand more fully how God hates for His children to judge and criticize others. We will also look at the consequences of these destructive mindsets.

1. In your dictionary, look up the word *judge* or *judgment* and the word *critical*. Record your insights.

2. Read Matthew 7:1–5. What does Jesus warn about judging?

   I think we definitely see the principle of sowing and reaping in this verse. If you and I sow judgment, we will reap judgment. Many times, we are reaping in our lives what we have sown into the lives of others.

3. Staying with Matthew 7:1–5, how does Jesus say we judge others?

4. We need to examine our own life—not our brother's. The devil loves to keep us busy mentally judging the faults of others. He knows that as long as we are busy judging others, we will not take time to examine our own faults.

5. Why do you think it is so easy to see the faults of others and not our own?

6. Read verse 5. What does Jesus call the person who is judging? How large is his sin compared to his brother's?

7. Have you ever found yourself judging and criticizing someone else for the same things you have done?

8. According to Romans 2:1–3, how does Paul admonish them for judging?

   When you and I judge others, we set our own standards of righteousness by which we judge, making ourselves guilty of being self-righteous. God judges according to His truth and His righteousness.

9. What does James 4:11–12 say we are really judging when we judge our brothers? How does he admonish us to change this type of thinking in verse 12?

10. Thank the Lord that He deals with us, not according to His justice but according to His mercy. What do we need to know about judging and showing mercy according to James 2:12–13?
11. What should our attitude about judging be according to Romans 14:1–5?
12. What things are we not to judge in others, according to Colossians 2:16–23?
13. How does Paul bottom line the problem of judging and being legalistic in Colossians 2:23?
14. Read 1 John 4:7–11. What principle do we need to appropriate for overcoming a judgmental spirit?

Judging and criticizing are fruits of the flesh. Love is the fruit of the Spirit. Love shows mercy and kindness to others. Wisdom from above is full of mercy and good fruits. One of God's greatest attributes toward us is His mercy. Praise God! God's mercy triumphs over His judgment. We all have weaknesses. We all make mistakes and have faults. Instead of condemning one another, let's show mercy and forgiveness toward each other. Paul exhorts us in Ephesians 5:1–2 to be imitators of God; forgiving one another, we are to walk in love. How about you? Do you want to be an imitator of your Heavenly Father by showing mercy? Or do you want to be an imitator of the devil and condemn and judge your brother?

Power Challenge

Ask God to show you any stinking thinking that might be present in your life and confess it to Him. If you have hurt others by being judgmental and critical (and they are aware of it) and if God leads you to do so, confess it also to them. God wants to clean up our thinking and remove those thought patterns that stink and are foul. God's ways are always the best. Thank God for Jeremiah 29:11 that you know that He thinks good thoughts toward you and that His desire is to prosper you, to give you hope, peace, and a future.

Meditate on Psalm 103:8–14. Thank Him for being so merciful and gracious to you.

Power Meditation

> "The Lord is gracious and full of compassion,
> slow to anger and great in mercy.
> The Lord is good to all,
> and His tender mercies are over all His works" (Psalm 145:8–9).

Chapter 6
Recognizing Wilderness Mindsets

Day 1: The Rebellious and Stubborn Mindset

Power Verse: "And the children of Israel said to [Moses and Aaron], 'Oh, that we had died by the hand of the Lord in the land of Egypt, when we sat by the pots of meat and when we ate bread to the full! For you have brought us out into this wilderness to kill this whole assembly with hunger." (Exodus 16:3)

The children of Israel are a good example of people suffering with a wilderness mindset. Not only did they wander in the wilderness for forty years, but they were a wilderness themselves. A wilderness is an unsettled, uncultivated, desolate region of land. The Israelites were people with uncultivated and desolate hearts because they knew about God but did not know Him personally. The children of Israel made the statement in today's Power Verse, only forty-five days after God so miraculously delivered them out of the hands of the Egyptians. Yet look at what they said that it would have been better to have died in Egypt, where at least they could have enjoyed one more pot of meat and one more piece of bread. God delivered them from the hands and Egyptian bondage of Pharaoh, but they were still in bondage to Egypt in their thinking. They were out of Egypt, but Egypt was still in them. They were unable to focus on the future that God had for them because they couldn't forget the past. They were filled with unbelief. They refused to trust and obey God even after experiencing His awesome miracles.

What should have been an eleven-day trip to the Promised Land became a forty-year journey. Most of that generation died before entering the land. Why? Take a look at the people. We see a people who were disobedient, complainers, ungrateful, stubborn, full of unbelief, and unwilling to let go of the past. As sad as that sounds, what is even more sad is that this wilderness mindset is prevalent in the church today.

If any of these mindsets describe you, or you feel like you have been wandering around in the wilderness for too long, be encouraged. God wants to set you free and give you hope for a better future. He can and will if we allow the Holy Spirit and the Word of God to shovel up the weeds and break the hardened soil in our hearts so He will have room to do what He wants to do in us—something fresh.

This week, we will examine the Word of God to evaluate thinking and attitudes of rebelliousness, stubbornness, grumbling and complaining, unbelief, ungratefulness, self-will, and the inability to let go of the past. Most often we are best able to recognize these mindsets during times of testing and transition—when God is trying to move us in a new direction. God doesn't take us into the wilderness to leave us there. His plan is to bless us and to take us to a better place.

Psalm 81:11–12 tells us that the children of Israel would not listen to God, "But My people would not heed My voice, and Israel would have none of Me, so I gave them over to their own stubborn heart, to walk in their own counsels." They would not obey Him, so He gave them over to follow their own stubborn ways. What a dangerous thing it is for a Christian to choose to disobey God to the point that He turns that person over to their own desires. Proverbs 14:12 says, "There is a way which seems right to a man, but its end is the way of death." God wants us to walk in His ways because His ways are the right ways. He will give us guidance, wisdom, strength, and protection when we choose His paths.

The principle we will look at today and throughout the week is that God blesses obedience, and there are consequences for disobedience. Remember: Wilderness mindsets are all rooted in disobedience.

1. Read Psalm 81:10–16. How does God describe the children of Israel in verses 11–13?

2. Why did God give them over to their own stubborn hearts?

3. According to verses 10,14, and 16, how did God say He would bless them if they obeyed?

4. Examine your life. Are there areas where you are not listening to the counsel of the Lord?

5. In chapters 12–16 of Exodus, we find the account of God delivering the children of Israel out of the hands of Pharaoh, the parting of the Red Sea, and God's bringing them safely through on dry land. God then leads them to the Wilderness of Shur. Read Exodus 15:22–26. According to verse 25, what did God say that He was going to do with the children of Israel?

6. What was God's test & promises in Exodus 15:26?

7. How have you handled times of testing from God? Are you trusting and obeying Him? Or are you stubbornly trying to find your own way?

8. According to Exodus 16:4, what was the test from God and what did God want to prove by testing them in the wilderness?

9. What was God testing them for in Exodus 20:20?

10. Describe some of the tests from God in your own life. What was God trying to teach you through testing?

11. Read Deuteronomy 8:1–9. According to verse 1, why were the children of Israel to be careful to observe God's commandments?

12. According to Deuteronomy 8:2, who led the children of Israel for forty years? What was the purpose?

13. Record your insights from Deuteronomy 8:3, what did God want them to understand about feefing them manna?

14. What was God's plan of blessings that He had in store for them according to Deuteronomy 8:7–9?

15. Can you think of times when you forfeited God's blessings to have your own way?

16. God wanted to be more important to them than entering into the Promised Land. We need to ask ourselves: Are the comforts and conveniences of this life more important to us than our relationship with God?

17. The author of the book of Hebrews—written to the Jewish believers in the early church—recounts the wilderness journey of the Israelites in chapters 3 and 4. According to chapter 3, verses 8–15, what warning does he give the church concerning rebellion?

18. How do you think that refusing to hear God's voice can lead to a hardened heart?

    Rebellion and stubbornness always lead to disobedience. The children of Israel heard God's Word, but they refused to believe Him. They were openly defiant toward God's authority and resisted His direction and control in their lives. The children of Israel were headstrong and determined to have their own way. They always went astray in their hearts, so God ultimately turned them over to follow their own stubborn ways. Because of their unbelief, God swore in His wrath that they wouldn't enter the Promised Land. How about you? Have you been missing God's Promised Land of rest and blessings because of a rebellious and stubborn heart?

Power Challenge

If you have recognized rebellious and stubborn mindsets in your life that have kept you from entering into God's Promised Land of rest, be encouraged. God loves you unconditionally and with an everlasting love. God hates sin, but He loves the sinner. He stands ready to forgive you and desires nothing more than for you to enter His rest. Hebrews 4:9–11 says that there remains a rest for the people of God. For he who has entered God's rest has himself also ceased from his works just as God did from His. Ask God to show what works you are to cease from so that you can enter His rest. Purpose in your heart that you want God to instruct you in His ways and that, by the power of the Holy Spirit, you want to be obedient to His ways. Obedience is doing what God wants you to do, in His way and in His time. Obedience brings rest to our souls. Disobedience brings restlessness to our souls.

Power Meditation

> "Come to Me, all you who labor and are heavy laden, and I will give you rest. Take My yoke upon you and learn from Me, for I am gentle and lowly in heart, and you will find rest for your souls. For My yoke is easy and My burden is light" (Matthew 11:28–30).

Day 2: The Complaining Mindset

Power Verse: "Also Moses said, 'This shall be seen when the Lord gives you meat to eat in the evening, and in the morning bread to the full; for the Lord hears your murmurings which you make against Him. And what are we? Your murmurings are not against us but against the Lord.'" (Exodus 16:8)

When we constantly complain about our problems, we are actually complaining against the Lord. Whether we complain openly by our words or silently in our hearts, we are complaining about God by showing an ungrateful attitude. We usually complain when things don't go our way. We complain about our jobs, our spouses, our ministers, our children, our friends. The list goes on and on. The very things that God blesses us with become the source of our complaining.

Complaining is one of the disobedient acts that kept the children of Israel from going in and possessing the Promised Land and can keep us from going in and possessing the promises that God has for us. Complaining opened the door to the enemy to come in and destroy them. They should have been grateful for God's goodness. Instead, they complained, for which they paid the price. Until we learn to glorify God in our thinking and attitudes during times of testing, we will never be delivered and experience victory. Rather, we will continue to wander around in the wilderness. God isn't glorified by our suffering. He is glorified when we have a Godly attitude in times of suffering. God wants us to learn to trust Him with every detail of life and praise Him that He has the ability and resources to meet all our needs in His way and in His time.

Remember, complaining is music to the devil's ear. Complaining is to the devil what praise is to God. When we complain, we rob God of His glory and we give it to the devil. Today, we will study God's Word to see how we can move beyond complaining to trusting and praising God.

1. Look up the following words in either a Bible or regular dictionary and record their meanings.

   Complaining
   Grumbling
   Murmuring

2. Read Numbers 11:1 How does God view complaining & grumbling?

3. What circumstances in your own life lead you to complain?

4. We often complain about our relationships with others and those in authority over us. According to 1 Peter 2:12–18, what should our attitudes be toward the following?

   People
   Government
   Employers

5. Times of suffering often provide a source for complaining. According to 1 Peter 2:19–20, what attitude does God find commendable in suffering?

6. What are some steps we can take to overcome our temptation to complain as we follow Jesus's example of suffering in 1 Peter 2:21–24?

7. Instead of complaining about a brother or sister in Christ, what are we admonished to do according to Ephesians 4:1–3?

8. Jesus also was tested in the wilderness. Read Luke 4:1–4. What similarities do you see in the testing of Jesus and in the testing of the Israelites?

9. What devices did Satan use to tempt Jesus? How did Jesus overcome each temptation?

10. How can you use the above account of Jesus overcoming temptation in your own life when you're tempted to complain?

Jesus entrusted Himself to the Father and overcame temptation in the wilderness. He went to the cross to purchase our salvation. He died on that cross and was buried in a tomb. God raised Him from the dead, and He now lives to make intercession for you and me. He praised God and was raised from the dead. The Israelites complained and remained in the wilderness.

11. According to Philippians 2: 14–16, what are we instructed to do concerning complaining?

12. How do you think complaining keeps us from being the shining lights in the world that God wants us to be?

13. Instead of letting the problems of life lead us into complaining about them, Paul teaches a better way in Philippians 4:4–8. He instructs us to pray with thanksgiving in every circumstance. According to these verses, what steps are you going to take the next time you're tempted to complain?

14. Not only does God hate complaining, no one likes to be around people who complain all the time. Our words can be positive, life-building words, or they can be destructive words that tear down and destroy. According to Proverbs 18:21, what do our words have the power to do?

The children of Israel complained to Moses over and over again that they had been brought into the wilderness to die. I believe they spoke a self-fulfilled prophecy over themselves that, in fact, did come true. Most of them did die in the wilderness and never made it to the Promised Land. We see from their examples that Proverbs 18:21 is true. Life and death are in the power of the tongue.

Since it is not always easy to not complain, I encourage you to take your complaints to the Lord like King David. David said in Psalm 142, "pour out my complaint before Him; I declare before Him my trouble." In Psalm 55 and Psalm 102, David makes his complaints known to God. Let me encourage you to follow David's example the next time you're tempted to complain. Talk to God. He is big enough to handle your complaints and to do something about them. Instead of going to the phone—go to the throne!

15. How has God spoken to you today?

Power Challenge

If you have recognized the mindset of complaining in your life, be encouraged. God can deliver you! It will take work on your part and lots of praying, praising, and confessing. In my own Christian walk, I have struggled for many years to overcome negative thinking. Complaining is a mindset that I am overcoming as well. This is a thought pattern that will keep us going backward instead of forward in our Christian walk. If you have a problem in this area, confess it to the Lord and receive His forgiveness, healing, and cleansing. Ask God to give you an attitude of gratitude and to fill your heart and mind with thanksgiving and praise. At the first opportunity to complain, choose to remember the goodness of God and to praise Him for His mercy and grace. When someone offends you, choose to take your complaint to God. Ask the Lord to empower you to praise Him daily and to be a shining light for Him everywhere you go.

Power Meditation

"He has put a new song in my mouth — praise to our God; many will see it and fear and will trust in the Lord.
Blessed is the man who makes the Lord his trust..."
(Psalms 40:3–4).

Day 3: The Forgetful Mindset

Power Verse: "Beware that you do not forget the Lord your God by not keeping His commandments, His judgments, and His statutes which I command you today, lest—when you have eaten and are full, and have built beautiful houses and dwell in them; and when your herds and your flocks multiply, and your silver and your gold are multiplied, and all that you have is multiplied; when your heart is lifted up, and you forget the Lord your God who brought you out of the land of Egypt, from the house of bondage." (Deuteronomy 8:11–14)

We need to remember and not forget the ways of God. Forgetfulness was a major problem with the children of Israel, and forgetfulness is also a common thread that runs through the church today. God led the Israelites through the wilderness for forty years, and He miraculously provided food, water, clothing, shelter, and protection from their enemies. Yet it seems the children of Israel suffered from amnesia. They quickly forgot God's faithfulness and goodness toward them. They forgot all the mighty miracles He performed. Moses reminded them over and over not to forget God when they crossed over into the Promised Land. God knew their hearts. He knew they would be tempted to forget Him in the midst of all the blessings. All the natural products of the Promised Land were to be gratefully recognized as blessings from God just as the manna provided to them supernaturally was a blessing from God. He did not want living in ease and prosperity to dull their awareness of the Lord, their God. Moses warned them against allowing their hearts to be filled with pride as they forgot the days of slavery, thirst and scorpions and when divine intervention was required for survival.

The truth God wanted to teach them in the wilderness when their stomachs were empty was the same truth He wanted to teach them in the Promised Land when their stomachs were full. That truth was: God and God alone is the source of their lives. In Deuteronomy 8:3, God says man does not live by bread alone but by every word that proceeds out of the mouth of God.

Today, we want to evaluate our own lives to see if we may be suffering from a forgetful mindset. We must remember that God is our Source. He is the Source of our salvation. He is the Source of our strength. He is the very Source of our lives. Blessings and prosperity flow into our lives from our Father in Heaven. We need to remember that God is sovereign. He is in control of every detail of our lives. He is all sufficient and has all power, ability, and resources to supply all our needs.

1. Record a definition and your insight for the following words.

   Forget
   Remember

2. Read Deuteronomy 8:7–20. In your own words, using today's terminology, how would you describe the Promised Land as Moses described it to the children of Israel in verses 7–9?

3. What instruction were they given in verse 10? What were they to be aware of in verses 11–14?

4. According to verses 11, 17, how do we forget God?

5. These warnings are for us today too. Why do you think that, in times of blessings, we need to be careful not to forget God?

6. As God blesses our lives, what attitudes do we need to guard against, as seen in verses 14, 17?

7. God wants us to have a humble attitude toward blessing and prosperity and not an attitude of pride. Pride causes our hearts to be raised up, and before too long, we begin to think that our blessings have come from our own hands. The humble person remembers God is his source and sufficiency. The proud person is self-sufficient and self-reliant, taking full credit for all he or she possesses. According to verse 18, what does God want us to remember when it comes to wealth and prosperity?

8. When we focus our eyes on our blessings, instead of the Blesser, we have a tendency to forget God. God doesn't have a problem with us having possessions as long as our possessions don't have us. According to verses 19–20, what results when we forget God?

9. We need to evaluate our own lives for ways that we forget God.

We can allow our lives to become so busy that we forget to spend time in God's Word. We forget to pray. We forget to thank Him and praise Him for His goodness. Anything that we put in first place in our lives ahead of God will soon lead us to forgetting to walk in God's ways. We forget God when we use human reasoning and understanding in making decisions, rather than relying on His wisdom. When we try to meet our needs in our own way in our own time with our own resources, we are forgetting God. God warned the children of Israel they would perish if they forgot the Lord their God and followed after other gods. We must be careful and hear that same warning. We may not make other gods out of wood or stone, but we can make gods out of other things in our lives. Anything we put above God can become a god to us. Our lives, our marriages, our relationships, our health, and our dreams can be destroyed if we forget to put God first place in our lives.

Are there areas in your life where you are forgetting God? Do you have gods in your life that are taking the place of the true and living God?

10. In Psalm 103, we are told to bless the Lord and forget not all His benefits. A benefit is something that promotes or enhances well-being in our lives. It is something that helps and aids us in doing what God has called us to do. Read Psalm 103:1–10. List all of the Lord's benefits that we should not forget.

11. God is the Source of all our blessings. He is the Source of our forgiveness, healing, redemption, strength, and satis-

THE POWER IN THINKING GOD'S WAY

faction. According to Proverbs 3:1–2, what will remembering God's Word produce in our lives?

12. How can we benefit from not forgetting God's wisdom, according to Proverbs 4:5–13?

13. Many of us live as if we were permanent fixtures upon this earth. We spend too much time thinking and meditating on temporal things, which are passing away, instead of things that have eternal value. God tells us in Psalm 31:15 that our days and times are in His hands. Time is a gift from God. We can either invest our time in things that have eternal consequence, or we can spend our time on those things that will soon be gone. We need to remember that God has a plan for each of our lives, and He only gives us a certain span of time upon this earth in which to accomplish His plans. Read the following verses, and record what it is we need to remember about our time here on earth.

Psalm 39:4–6
Psalm 90:12
Psalm 103:14–16
Job 8:9
Job 14:5

14. David prayed that God would enable him to understand the frailty and brevity of life so that He could gain wisdom to discern the true meaning of life. Compared to God's timelessness, a lifespan of even eighty or ninety is pitifully short. We need to remember that life is brief, and God wants us to invest our time in things that will store up treasures for us and others in His Kingdom. If you knew that the Lord was going to return tomorrow, how would you spend your time today?

15. One of the most important things that a Christian needs to remember is that Jesus is coming soon, and we need to be ready for His appearing. One of the next unfulfilled Bible

prophesies to take place is the rapture of the Church. Read 1 Thessalonians 4:16–18. Write these verses word for word.

16. How can living in the light of the soon return of Jesus Christ help us to not become forgetful concerning the things of God?

Power Challenge

Let's summarize the truths from God's Word that we don't want to forget.

Remember:

> God is our Source–God is the Source of life.
> He is the Source of the length of our days.
> God is the Source of our salvation.
> He delivered us out of bondage to sin.
> God is the Source of our satisfaction.
> He satisfies our mouth with good things.
> God is the Source of all blessing and prosperity.
> He gives us power to gain wealth.
> God is the Source of our redemption.
> He will catch us up in the clouds of glory!

Power Meditation

> "Looking for the blessed hope and glorious appearing of our great God and Savior Jesus Christ, who gave Himself for us, that He might redeem us from every lawless deed and purify for Himself His own special people, zealous for good works" (Titus 2:3–14).

Day 4: Minding the Past

Power Verse: "'Why has the Lord brought us to this land to fall by the sword, that our wives and children should become victims? Would it not be better for us to return to Egypt!' So they said to one another, 'Let us select a leader and return to Egypt.'" (Numbers 14:3–4)

The children of Israel could not quit thinking about where they had come from long enough to get to where they were going. We can see from their words that they weren't trusting in God. They were so filled with failure and negativity that they were already determined to fail. The Israelites continually looked at and talked about how things were in Egypt. God brought them out of Egypt to take them to the Promised Land. He wanted them to look at where He was taking them and to take their eyes off where they had been. They based everything in their lives on what they had known in Egypt and on what they could see with their natural eyes. The children of Israel had no faith, vision, or hope for a better future.

When we allow our past to determine our present and our future, we are living with a wilderness mindset that will keep us bound and unable to move ahead to experience victory in our lives. The children of Israel had been delivered from a place of bondage and slavery, but they wanted to go back to that life because it was familiar and comfortable. We need to be careful that we don't forfeit a bright future because we are unwilling to let go of the past. Whether it is past failures or past successes that keep us bound, we need to move on and experience the good things that God has planned for our lives.

Today, we will learn from God's Word how we can have victory overcoming our past.

1. List any areas of your past that you still struggle with.
2. If we measure our future by our past, we are setting ourselves up to repeat it. Continually looking back at our yesterdays, analyzing our failures, mistakes, abuse, or even successes will not prevent us from making the same mistakes. The devil loves to keep us bound up in the lies and

guilt from the past. He wants to move us backward, but God wants us to move forward. We must treat our past the way God treats it. According to Philippians 3:13–16, what steps does God give us for dealing with our past?

3. Have you been forgetting what is behind so as to press on toward what is ahead? Or have you been pressing for what is behind, thus forgetting what is ahead?

   God never goes back. He is always looking ahead, and He wants us to move beyond our past and, while enjoying the present, move forward to what He has ahead for us. The past is gone. No matter how terrible or how wonderful it was—it is gone. Don't live in the past and let it drain you of your life in the present.

4. How does God describe the future that He has planned for us according to Jeremiah 29:11?

   Notice that God does not outline the plan. Nor does He say, "You will know the plan." Only God knows the plan—and it is good.

5. Do you evaluate new opportunities and challenges based on your past experiences? Or do you view new opportunities and challenges as God wanting to do something new and exciting in your life that will stretch you?

6. How does Isaiah 42:9 and 43:18–19 show us God's desire to do something new in our lives? How will we know when He is ready to do it?

7. What former things have come to pass in your life that you need to let go of so that you can take hold of new things that God wants to do?

   God's faithfulness to supply His former grace, mercy, favor, and blessings in our lives should encourage us to hope in His future provisions as well. God is constant in His care for His children, and His mercies and compassion are still new each day (Lamentations 3:23).

8. The only aspect to our past that God wants us to remember is His faithfulness to care and provide for us. Those challenging times and decisions back in the past that God

so graciously led us through should remind us that He will also be with us in the present and future as we face new challenges. What does Hebrews 13:8 show us about God's character?

9. In Isaiah, chapters 52–54, we see the captivity of the children of Israel. They had been taken captive because they had forsaken God to follow after idols. In their hopelessness, they were fearful that God would never forgive their sins and iniquity. All they could see were their failures. God spoke to them in Isaiah 54:4–8 about their situation. Read this passage and record your insights on how God dealt with their shame.

   God did not say, "I want you to remember your shame and learn from it." No, He said, "Forget it." He had forgotten it, and He said He would not let them be ashamed, disgraced, or humiliated. He said, "I won't remind you of your past, so don't let anyone else remind you—forget about it!"

10. The good news of the Gospel is that Christ frees us from the past and gives us new life in Him. According to 2 Corinthians 5:17–21, how has Jesus dealt with our past?

   God, who raised Jesus from the dead, has raised every believer to a new life in Him. That doesn't mean that deep wounds and guilt automatically disappear, but it does mean that we have power and freedom to overcome them. In John 11, we have the account of Jesus raising Lazarus from the dead. Jesus called out to Lazarus to come forth, and Lazarus came forth. Jesus then instructed those watching to lose him of his grave clothes and to let him go. God is saying to many of us that it is time to be free of those old grave clothes and start enjoying the new creations we are in Jesus Christ. We don't have to be bound by those grave clothes of the past because Jesus has given us new garments to wear. He has given us His robes of righteousness to wear. As 2 Corinthians 5:21 says, "For He made Him who knew no sin to be sin for us, that we might become the righteousness of God in Him."

Power Challenge

Pray and ask God to show you if you are being bound by grave clothes of the past. Sometimes, we bury things so deep that it is difficult for us to discern the truth about ourselves. Ask the Holy Spirit to shine His search light on your heart to reveal any past hurts, lies, guilt, or unforgiveness that you need to deal with in order for God to loose you from them. Perhaps you have believed the lie that because you haven't been happy in the past, you will never be happy. Perhaps you keep evaluating what God is doing in your life today based on how He did things in the past. Quit putting God in a box. He is a great and mighty God who has good plans for your life. Allow Him to move in your life in a fresh new way. He is just waiting for you to ask!

Power Meditation

"Therefore, if the Son makes you free, you shall be free indeed" (John 8: 36).

Day 5: The Mindset of Discontentment

Power Verse: "They wandered in the wilderness in a desolate way; they found no city to dwell in. Hungry and thirsty, their soul fainted in them... Oh, that men would give thanks to the Lord for His goodness, and for His wonderful works to the children of men! For He satisfies the longing soul and fills the hungry soul with goodness." (Psalm 107: 4–5, 8–9)

We have seen how the children of Israel were a stubborn, complaining, forgetful race of people. They were unable to stop talking about their past, and they were never content with anything. God fed them supernatural manna from heaven, yet they weren't satisfied. They wanted meat. We see their discontentment in that they complained about everything.

Usually, when we are not content, we complain more. Many times, we want God to bless us with more when, in fact, we aren't even content with what He has already given us. God delivered the children of Israel out of bondage to lead them to the Promised Land of blessing and freedom. He had to take them through wilderness, testing first in order to teach them to trust and obey Him. He wanted to satisfy the longing of their souls with Himself. He was trying to teach them that He was their Source and that He alone was their sufficiency. For forty years, God tried to teach them that man does not live by bread alone but by every word that proceeds from the Word of God. What should have been an eleven-day trip became a forty-year journey in the wilderness. Sometimes, God has to take us through wilderness testing to break off the shackles of sin in our lives. He wants to deliver us from the stronghold that the world has on our thinking and attitudes. Discontentment is a result of self-centeredness and an ungrateful attitude toward the goodness of God.

If you are experiencing a lot of discontentment in your life, you are living with a wilderness mindset that keeps you from really enjoying the life that God wants you to have. Contentment comes to our lives as we submit to God and His plans and as we learn to rely upon God for every need.

Contentment comes when we keep our eyes focused on Him and off ourselves and others. We will enjoy contentment as we learn to practice an attitude of gratitude. Misplaced priorities can rob us of contentment. God wants us to experience contentment. Contentment is not something so elusive it can't be attained. Whether you consider yourself fairly content or view yourself struggling to find contentment, our study today will help give you confidence and hope.

1. Look up the definition for contentment and record your insights.
2. Following is a list of areas where each of us has concerns, in one form or another. From 1 to 10 (with 1 being the lowest and 10 being the highest), record your level of contentment in each of these areas.

Relationship with God
Relationship with husband
Relationship with children

Relationship with friends
Career
Finances
Physical appearance, weight
Material possessions
Use of gifts and talents
Use of time
Church
Present stress level

God wants us to be content with ourselves. So many Christians don't love and accept themselves completely. The foundation of our contentment rests in knowing who we are in Christ and that we are loved and totally accepted by God.

3. Describe the attitudes the following people had about themselves. Also record God's response to their feelings of inadequacy or weakness about themselves.

Sarah (Genesis 18:9–15; 21:1–7)
Gideon (Judges 6:11–18)
Mary (Luke 1:26–31)

4. How does God want us to view ourselves according to Ephesians 1:3–14?

5. Wrong thinking—comparing ourselves to others' gifts, talents, and abilities—can rob us of contentment. According to 1 Corinthians 12:14–27, what is the proper view that God wants us to have of ourselves as related to the body of Christ?

6. How can having the understanding and knowledge that you are a significant part of the body of Christ help you to find more contentment with yourself?

7. When we have difficulties in accepting ourselves, we form an attitude that can lead to a lack of contentment. How

can I learn contentment in light of the truth in Psalm 139:13–16?

8. Keeping our peace and contentment in times of trials is difficult for most of us. In what areas at the present time are you experiencing trials? What is your contentment level?

9. Rebekah experienced a trial as she saw her husband Isaac plan to give the inheritance to their son Esau when she wanted it given to Jacob. Read Genesis 25:22–23. What was the prophecy that God had given to Rebekah concerning her two sons?

10. Instead of trusting God concerning the inheritance, how did Rebekah handle this situation, according to Genesis 27:1–10?

11. What was the price of Rebekah taking matters into her own hands and deceiving Isaac, according to Genesis 27:41–42?

12. By practicing the truth from Psalm 37:23–26, how can these steps help us to have contentment during trials?

13. According to Philippians 4:11–13, what things had Paul learned about being content?

14. Paul said that he had learned to be content. Contentment isn't something we get going through prayer lines or having hands laid on us. According to Paul, contentment is something we learn. List circumstances that have come up in your life that have taught you how to be content.

15. Finances are another area that can bring discontentment into our lives. We hear so many prosperity messages today that it is easy for us to become discontented. What wisdom and insight can we gain concerning wealth, and what principles for contentment can we learn from the following verses?

    Ecclesiastes 5:10–12
    Proverbs 11:4, 28
    1 Timothy 6:6–11

16. What instruction is given to the rich in 1 Timothy 6:17–19?

17. What instruction does Jesus give us concerning wealth and possessions in Luke 12:15?

18. In Luke 12:16–21, we have Jesus's parable of the rich fool. What was the rich man's problem? Where did he place his faith?

According to verse 21, what are we to be rich in?

19. What promise can we claim from Philippians 4:19 to help us learn contentment?

20. Where are you placing your thoughts—on your needs or on your wants?

21. How has God spoken to you today?

Power Challenge

Write down any areas of discontentment in your life. It may be in your health, finances, stress, relationships with your friends or your spouse. Whatever it may be, give it to God and allow Him to work in the situation. Ask God to show you if there is something you need to do or change that would improve that particular area of your life. If it is something that requires you to wait on the Lord, pray that God would help you to wait patiently and peacefully upon Him as He works everything out in His way and His time. Sometimes, our lack of contentment is a result of wrong thinking and attitudes that result in wrong choices. Review the following areas that may be culprits in robbing your contentment. Pray and ask God to help you answer each question honestly.

Are you submitted to God's plan for your life?

Are you totally trusting and relying on God to provide for your needs?

Are you comparing yourself to others?

Are you trying to earn God's acceptance by your performance?

Are you placing too much trust and faith in money and
material things?

Are you placing too much importance on your appearance?

Are you using your spiritual gifts to serve God?

Are you appreciative of the relationships in your life?

Are you organized and a good steward of your time?

Are you grateful most of the time? Or are you ungrateful
most of the time?

Pray and commit those problem areas to the Lord and ask Him
to help you learn to be content as you allow Him to work in your
life. Thank God for His Word that is like a mirror, always showing
us where we need to improve. Praise God for His grace that gives us
the power and strength to improve.

Power Meditation

"But godliness with contentment is great gain"
(1 Timothy 6:6).

JUDY GOLIGHTLY

Chapter 7
Overcoming a Martha Mentality

Power Verse: "Do not fret—it only causes harm." (Psalm 37:8)

In Luke 10:41–42, Jesus and His disciples had come to eat at Martha and Mary's home, and we see a contrast between Martha and her sister, Mary. "And Jesus said to her, 'Martha, Martha, you are worried and troubled about many things. But one thing is needed, and Mary has chosen that good part, which will not be taken away from her." Mary sat at the feet of Jesus to hear His Word. She showed a readiness to receive His Word and to submit to it. Martha, on the other hand, was busy making everything perfect for Jesus's visit. She wanted to entertain Jesus with style. Instead of enjoying Jesus, she let the care of preparing the food and preparing her home become a burden that troubled and worried her.

Just imagine if you knew that you would be entertaining Jesus in your home tonight. Would you be composed when He arrived? Or would you be stressed out because you had worked all day trying to make everything perfect down to the gnat's eyelash? Martha wanted to please Jesus. She wanted to make everything just right for Him. But in the process, she became frazzled and complained to Jesus that Mary was doing nothing to help her. Jesus rebuked her in a loving and kind way. Martha had focused on the temporal things of life. Mary had her eyes focused on those things with eternal value. Being worried and troubled about things of this world are common among Christians today.

God doesn't want us to worry and be troubled with the cares of this life. Worry paralyzes us and keeps us from being effective in our ministries to the Lord Jesus Christ. We can become so busy serving the Lord that we forget to sit at His feet and listen to His Word. If you are suffering with a Martha mentality with thinking patterns of worry, anxiety, busyness, distraction, and perfectionism, be encouraged! This lesson will help you be an overcomer with answers from God's Word.

Day 1: The Worried Mind

Power Verse: "And Jesus answered and said to her, 'Martha, Martha, you are worried and troubled about many things. But one thing is needed, and Mary has chosen that good part, which will not be taken away from her.'" (Luke 10:41–42)

W. R. Inge has said that worry is interest paid on trouble before it falls due (London Observer, February 14, 1932). As I write this study, I am reminded of how qualified I am to discuss this topic. For most of my life, I worried and fretted about everything. I was addicted to worry—and it wore me out!

Worry will rob us of joy and peace in our lives and keep us from enjoying the abundant life that Jesus came to give us. We worry about our kids, our health, our jobs, our finances, even our death. The list goes on and on. Worry is a sin and is evidence of our lack of faith in God. Worry is a sin because when we worry, we are putting our faith in what we worry about rather than placing our faith in God.

Worry erases the promises of God from our mind. It is an attack on our mind from the devil that keeps us distracted and prevents us from serving the Lord. It is impossible to walk with peace and joy and be filled with worry. Webster's Dictionary defines worry as "to feel uneasy or troubled; to cause to feel anxious and distressed; a source of nagging concern; to torment oneself with disturbing thoughts." God never intended for His children to sit around tormenting their minds with disturbing thoughts. Yet that is what we do by worrying. Let's look at God's Word today to gain understanding and insight about how to stop worrying and how to walk in peace.

1. List the areas in your life that cause you to worry.
2. Do you worry occasionally, often or addictively?

3. What do you usually do to ease or eliminate your worry?

4. Read Matthew 6:25–34. According to verses 25, 31, and 34, what does Jesus command us to not worry about?

5. What important principle does Jesus give about worrying in these three verses?

6. How does God assure them that He will meet their needs, according to verses 26–30?

7. Do you worry about your needs being met? Are you able to enjoy life from day to day? Or do you spend too much time worrying about tomorrow?

8. What does worry not do, according to verse 27?

9. Worry will never add years to our lives. Indeed, it will take away years. Worry never changes anything. It only makes things worse. According to verses 32–33, what does Jesus admonish us to do concerning our worrying about our needs being met?

10. In verse 32, God points out that His children are not to be like the world. The world seeks after things. We are to seek the Lord. He has promised that if we will do that, He will give us all the things He knows we need. God intends for us to live and enjoy an abundant life. According to John 10:10, what does the enemy do to thwart the abundant life that Jesus gave us?

11. As you reflect on your own life, what areas has the enemy tried to destroy through worry?

   If we are going to live in peace, we must make a choice not to worry. We can choose to worry about everything, or we can choose to have peace instead. Peace is a fruit of the Spirit (Galatians 5:22). Fruit is a result of abiding in the vine. If we want to have peace and experience rest in our souls, we must abide in the Lord.

12. Read John 15:4–5, who is the vine, and who are the branches?

13. Abide means to live and dwell in. According to John 15:10, why is it important for you and I to abide in Jesus? What will that produce in our lives?

14. According to verse 10, how do we abide in Jesus? Are you daily abiding in the vine by keeping God's commands about not worrying?

    In John 15:11, Jesus said, "These things I have spoken to you, that My joy may remain in you, and that your joy may be full."

15. Peace and joy are fruits of the Spirit that will help us overcome worry. Are these fruits evident in your life?

    How do we abide in the Vine? We abide in the Lord as we draw near to Him, asking for strength, wisdom, guidance, and direction and as we hide God's Word in our hearts and appropriate the Word in every circumstance of life. In times of trouble, we need to meditate on the promises of God and stand firm. Don't dwell on the problem. Dwell on the Problem-solver. Meditating on the promises of God and His attributes will help us overcome worry.

16. Read Romans 8:26–39. List all the ways and promises of God that encourage us not to worry but to trust that God is in control.

17. Isaiah 9: 6 says that Jesus is the Prince of Peace. What three things does Jesus say in John 16:33 that can help us to overcome worry?

    We must remember to believe what God says in His Word. Jesus said in John 16:33, "I have spoken to you." Jesus's Words can give us peace even in the midst of our world of tribulation. We must choose to take to heart His Word that says, "Be of good cheer," because He has overcome the world. Peace is not the absence of problems but a freedom from disquieting feelings and thoughts in the midst of problems because we are abiding in the Prince of Peace.

18. Jesus said in John 14:26 that He was sending us the Holy Spirit Who would teach us and bring all His Words to our remembrance. What does He want us to remember in John 14:26–29? What do you think the link is between us simply having head knowledge about His peace and walking in His peace every day?

19. What is the link to appropriating joy and peace according to Romans 15:13?

    Every aspect of the Christian life is lived out by faith. Faith is believing God's Word in spite of feelings and circumstances. Believing is our link to receiving peace and joy from God. For the Christian to believe is to accept the Word of God as true and to receive it and submit to it. Worry is a sin. It shows that we are not believing God's report but that we are believing the report of our feelings and circumstances instead.

20. What can we learn about believing God from Mark 9:23 and Mark 11:24?

21. How has God spoken to you today? What attributes and beliefs do you need to change in order to overcome worry and live a life of peace and joy?

Power Challenge

Write Luke 10:41–42 on several 3 x 5 inches cards, replacing Martha's name with your name. Place one card in your car, one on your refrigerator, one by your bed, in your purse—wherever one is needed. Every time you start to worry, read that Scripture. Confess the sin of worry to God and ask Him to empower you to walk in His joy and peace. Make the decision today that you will not worry anymore! When you are tempted to worry over a particular situation, remember:

> Why worry when God has promised to provide all my needs?
> Why worry when I can pray?
> Why worry when God is for me?
> Why worry when God can't fail?
> Why worry when God will make a way?
> Why worry when God will guide and provide?
> Why worry when God is working all things together for my good?

Why worry when the Holy Spirit Himself intercedes for
me according to the will of God?
Why worry when God gives me peace?
Why worry when nothing is impossible for God?
Why worry when nothing is impossible if I believe in God?

Power Meditation

"The Lord will give strength to His people; the Lord
will bless His people with peace" (Psalm 29:11).

Day 2: The Anxious Mind

Power Verse: "Anxiety in the heart of man causes depression, but a
good word makes it glad." (Proverbs 12:25)

It seems that everyone is talking about anxiety and how they
have been affected by it.

> Anxiety is a state of uneasiness and apprehension
> due to uncertainty. It is fear resulting from the
> anticipation of a threatening event or situation.
> Anxiety suggests feelings of fear and apprehen-
> sion. It is characterized by increased pulse rate
> and blood pressure, quickened breathing, per-
> spiration and dryness of the mouth. Anxiety is
> an element of many psychic disorders including
> phobias, panic attacks and obsessive-compulsive
> disorders. (Microsoft Book Shelf Dictionary)

There are literally hundreds of anti-anxiety drugs on the mar-
ket today to relieve symptoms associated with anxiety. The Body of
Christ is not immune from anxiety.

I have been affected by anxious thoughts many times to the
point that I have experienced an anxiety attack. How frightening.
You're simply talking to someone, and suddenly, you feel like your
life is draining from you. You feel a total lack of control. Through

applying God's Word to those areas that create anxious thoughts in me, I have been successful in overcoming anxiety attacks.

Solomon was the wisest man who ever lived, and he understood anxiety. He knew that an anxious heart would lead a man to depression. He also knew that a good word could turn an anxious heart into a glad heart. As Christians, we need to get back to the good word—the Word of God. The Word of God is the medicine we need to cure anxiety. The Bible is written by our Creator to His creation. It is His working manual for us on how we are to live and how we are to deal with anxiety. God never intended for His children to be anxious about life.

Anxiety literally paralyzes us from living and from becoming all that God has created us to be. An anxious person is distressed, disturbed, worried, troubled, overly-concerned about many things, ill at ease, restless, and fretful. If any of these negative thoughts and emotions describe you, don't miss this lesson. Let's come and reason together as we find solutions to anxiety from God's Word. Let's see how we can overcome anxiety.

1. What events or activities trigger anxious thoughts for you?
2. From 1 to 10 (with 1 being the lowest and 10 being the highest), rate the following as to the level of anxiety they produce in your life:

____Your health	____Going to the doctor
____Going to the dentist	____The health of family members
____Flying	____Starting a new job
____Entertaining	____Your relationship with God
____When your plans change suddenly	____The future
____Move to a new city	____Praying
____Making new friends	____Your son or daughter getting a driver's license

3. God knew that we would experience anxiety, and it is comforting to know that He understands our anxious thoughts. It is encouraging to know that as we apply the following Scriptures to our lives, we can overcome anxiety.

    Isaiah 43:1–3
    Isaiah 41:10
    Psalm 94:18–19
    Psalm 138:7–8

4. According to Psalm 37:7–8, what should we not fret over? What does fretting do, according to verse 8?
5. How has anxiety been harmful in your life?
6. Instead of fretting, what are we instructed to do in Psalm 37:7?
7. One of the ways we rest in the Lord is by letting Him carry our burdens. Read Psalm 55:22 and 1 Peter 5:6–7. What does it mean to you to cast our cares and our anxieties on the Lord?
8. Praying enables us to enter God's rest and to experience His peace. What does Philippians 4:6–7 instruct us to do concerning prayer? What is the promise we can claim?
9. Paul says that we are to pray about everything. Nothing in our life is too big or too insignificant for God. Most of the time, it is the small things in life that drive us crazy. Do you take everything to God in prayer? Or do you only pray about those things that you think are big and important?
10. Do you pray with thanksgiving—thanking God for the resources, power, and desire to meet your every need? Are you praying with confidence that if God said He would do something, He will do it?
11. God tells us not to be anxious but pray instead. He promised that when we do, He will guard our hearts and minds with a peace that surpasses all human understanding. Philippians 4:8–9 gives us wonderful insight as to what we should do after praying. According to these verses, what should we choose to think upon?

12. According to Matthew 11:28–30, what does Jesus tell us to do in order to have rest and be free of anxious thoughts?

13. From the above Scripture, what words are used to tell us that Jesus's rest is ours but that it is our choice to receive it?

Are you coming to Jesus for rest?

14. Anxious thoughts have become a stronghold for many of us. Anxiety is a weapon the devil uses to attack our minds and to keep us paralyzed from moving out in faith and accomplishing all that God has ordained us to do. According to 2 Corinthians 10:4–5, what are we to do with anxious thoughts that have become strongholds?

We must never forget that we are in a spiritual battle in this Christian life—a battle between the flesh, the spirit, and the devil. Second Corinthians 10:4–5 tells us that God has empowered us with divine weapons mighty in Him for the pulling down of strongholds. We are instructed to bring those anxious thoughts captive to the Lord Jesus Christ. James 4:7 says that we are to submit ourselves to God, resist the devil and he will flee.

Power Challenge

If you have identified anxiety in your life, whether occasionally or often, go to God with those thoughts. Talk to Him about them. Make it a daily habit to meditate on Philippians 4:6–8. God wants us to overcome anxiety and to experience His lasting and sustaining peace. The next time you find yourself getting anxious, stop and do the following.

1. Pray. Praise and worship God for all His goodness.
2. Make supplication. Talk to God about your circumstance.
3. Thank God for what He is doing in your life through that particular circumstance that makes you more into the image of Christ. Keep an attitude of gratitude; make a

choice to rejoice. Whatever we can thank God for, we can have peace about. Remember 1 Thessalonians 5:16–18, "Rejoice always, pray without ceasing, in everything give thanks; for this is the will of God for you in Christ Jesus."

4.   Get into the habit of Philippians 4:8-ing your thought life. Ask yourself, "Is what I'm thinking true, pure, holy, good, praiseworthy, etc.?"

5.   Daily line up your thinking with the Word of God and ask Him to help you recognize thoughts that are from the evil one and bring those thoughts captive to the Lord Jesus Christ.

If you and I will practice these principles from God's Word every day, we can experience God's lasting and sustaining peace and overcome anxiety in our lives.

Power Meditation

"You will keep him in perfect peace, whose mind is stayed on You, because he trusts in You" (Isaiah 26:3).

Day 3: The Busy and Distracted Mind

Power Verse: "Surely every man walks about like a shadow; surely they busy themselves in vain; he heaps up riches and does not know who will gather them." (Psalm 39:6)

We live in a busy world. There are schedules to keep, appointments to make, household chores to attend to, carpools to be driven, groceries to buy, calls to make, loved ones who need us, committees to serve on—on and on the list goes and grows. We keep ourselves so busy that if God wants to talk to us, He has to leave us a voice mail or e-mail to get our attention! God never intended for us to live on such a fast pace that we don't have time for Him, let alone ourselves. Obviously, we all have work that must get done, but our priorities need to be examined on a regular basis. When our priorities get out of order, we begin to do things that God never called us to do— and do them for all the wrong reasons. There are good things to get involved in, but they may not be "God's things." We need to evaluate the busyness in our lives to see if our activities are bringing health or leanness to our souls. We have a choice. We can live balanced lives or lives that are out of control because of busyness and distractions.

Today, we want to examine our lives to see if we are actively engaged in God's business or our own busyness. Are our lives busy or balanced? Busyness keeps us distracted to the point of losing sight of right priorities. Perhaps you need to overcome the "Busy Mind Syndrome."

1. Prayerfully, ask God to show you your priorities at the present time. Be honest and list your priorities in order of their importance to you.
2. As you live and plan your daily life, what are the warning signs that let you know that your life has become too busy?
3. According to Colossians 1:9–12, how did Paul pray for believers to have a balanced lifestyle?
4. We need to ask ourselves why we stay so busy. From the list below, check any possible reasons.

_____ Staying busy makes me feel worthwhile.
_____ Staying busy helps my self-esteem.
_____ Staying busy makes me feel needed.
_____ Staying busy keeps me from feeling guilty.
_____ Staying busy helps keep me from having to deal with difficult areas of my life.
_____ Staying busy gives me a sense of control over my life.
_____ Staying busy with church makes me feel more acceptable to God.
_____ I don't know how to say no.

5. How does staying too busy make you feel? Check the following that apply to you.

_____ Stressed   _____ Edgy
_____ Irritable   _____ Overwhelmed

_____ Frustrated   _____ Confused

_____ Fatigued   _____ Unfulfilled

_____ Angry   _____ Disconnected

6. Time is a gift from God. How we spend it is very important to Him. What insights can be learned about our time in Ephesians 5:15–17?

7. God wants us to be wise with our time. We can either spend our time with busy activities or accomplishing those things directed by the will of God. According to 1 Corinthians 3:10–15, how will the way we have spent our time here on earth be revealed at the Judgment Seat of Christ?

8. Only those things built on the foundation of Christ will not be burned up—things done according to the will of God in the power of the Holy Spirit. What works are you involved in that you think would be classified as hay, wood, and stubble? What things do you feel represent gold, silver, and precious stones?

9. Read the account of Martha and Mary in Luke 10:38–42. Study the contrast between the two sisters. Write in "Martha" or "Mary" beside the words below that best describe them. When completed, we will see a balanced life contrasted with an unbalanced life.

_____ Submitted   _____ Teachable

_____ Perfectionist   _____ Busy

_____ Complaining   _____ Joyful

_____ Worried   _____ Content

_____ Confident   _____ Learning

_____ Composed   _____ Judgmental

_____ Performance Oriented   _____ Free

_____ Enslaved   _____ Self-righteous

10. Looking at this list, are you a "Martha" or a "Mary?"

11. Jesus said that Mary had chosen "that good part, which will not be taken away from her." What is the "good part," according to Luke 10:39?

12. What do you think Jesus meant when He said this would not be taken away from Mary?

13. Do you read the Word of God? Or has your life become too busy and distracted?

14. According to Proverbs 2:6, what do we gain by spending time in God's Word?

15. According to Proverbs 4:7–8, what should we seek in God's Word?

16. We spend time in God's Word to gain wisdom, understanding, and knowledge. The fourth chapter of Proverbs tells us to embrace wisdom, and it will promote us in this life. Read Proverbs 2:10–12 and Proverbs 4:10–12. List all the benefits of gaining God's wisdom in this life.

17. Wisdom gained through God's Word will help us establish right priorities and will help us get off the fast track of busyness and discover more peace and quiet in our lives. To be quiet is to be still, peaceful, calm, and tranquil. It is the absence of noise, clutter, confusion, and agitation.

18. How has God spoken to you about your priorities today? What changes are necessary to make in your present schedule? Are you willing to make them?

Power Challenge

God wants to speak to all of us. However, at times, we allow our minds and schedules to become so busy that we can't hear the still, small voice of God. As a result, we become burned out, tired, frustrated, and unfulfilled. Instead of filling that vacuum in our lives with busy stuff, we must let God fill it with Himself. Beginning today, I want to challenge you to set ten minutes aside every day to sit quietly before God. During this time, don't pray or read your Bible. Prayerfully, ask God to empty your mind of every care and concern so that you can just be quiet and still and be able to hear

God's still, small voice. Ask the Lord to speak to you personally about your present priorities and time commitments. Ask Him to help you to be willing to make whatever changes He desires for you. We must choose quiet lives over busy lives if we are going to hear God's voice (1 Kings 19:11–13). Are you willing to do that?

Power Meditation

"Be still, and know that I am God" (Psalm 46:10).

Day 4: Overcoming the Legalistic and Self-righteous Mind

Power Verse: "Did you receive the Spirit by the works of the law, or by the hearing of faith? Are you so foolish? Having begun in the Spirit, are you now being made perfect by the flesh?" (Galatians 3:2–3)

Under the Old Covenant, the Israelites' relationship with God was based on keeping a strict set of rules. If they kept the law, they would be blessed. If they broke the law, they had to make sacrifices. The keeping of the law and making sacrifices were the only way to maintain a relationship with God.

Today, you and I can enjoy our relationship with God under the New Covenant. We have the wonderful gift of grace because of Jesus's sacrifice on the cross. Our relationship with God is no longer based on keeping certain rules—it is based on grace and grace alone.

Remember our earlier account of Martha and Mary? Mary understood her need to have a close personal relationship with Jesus. And she knew there was nothing she could do to earn it. Martha, on the other hand, had a self-righteous attitude. Romans 11:6 tells us that we are saved by grace. "And if by grace, then it is no longer of works; otherwise grace is no longer grace. But if it is of works, it is no longer grace."

Many Christians are bound to keeping certain religious regulations of their own making. Legalism is a real problem in the church today. We can become so legalistic that we make praying and reading the Bible a legalistic exercise. Discipline is something we need in our Christian walk, but we must avoid legalism. Sometimes, we get so caught up in obeying the rules and keeping the laws that we miss out on the personal relationship that God wants to have with us. He wants us to obey Him; however, He doesn't want us to get so caught up in keeping man-made rules that we forget to depend on Him.

Are you enjoying your relationship with God? Do you understand that your righteousness is in Christ? Or do you feel like God becomes angry at you every time you make a mistake? Let's overcome living in legalism and discover the joy of living in God's grace.

1. In your own words, describe the personality characteristics of a self-righteous and legalistic person.

2. Are you legalistic in some areas of your life? If yes, over what issues are you legalistic?

3. The Pharisees were the religious group of Jesus's day. They exercised a strict adherence to the keeping of the law and many other man-made religious codes. In Luke 18, Jesus tells the parable of the Pharisee and the tax collector. The tax collector represented the lowest of sinners in the Pharisee's eyes. Read Luke 18:9–14. According to verse 9, to whom was Jesus addressing this parable?

4. How did the Pharisee describe his righteous acts in Luke 18:10–12?

5. How did the tax collector describe his righteous acts in Luke 8:13?

6. According to Luke 18:14, whose righteousness did Jesus approve and why?

    God hates the sin of pride. The Pharisee was called prideful while the tax collector was called humble. The Pharisee was relying on his own ability to keep external laws rather than trusting in God. It never occurred to the Pharisee that he was a sinner just like the tax collector. Jesus said that the tax collector was justified because he was honest with God. He admitted that he was a sinner, and he realized that he needed God's mercy. He was justified before God because he was humble. The humble person realizes that they are nothing without God and that apart from His grace, they are lost sinners. Proud people are self-reliant, self-sufficient, and self-righteous. They think that their righteousness will impress God when, in fact, God hates self-righteousness because it is rooted in pride.

7. What about your own life? Are you following some religious code that you think will win God's approval? Or are you relying completely on His grace?

    The Pharisee judged the tax collector as being a sinner and thanked God that he (the Pharisee) wasn't like other sinful men.

    The Pharisee shows us that when we think we are better than other people or have greater moral and spiritual character than others, we are suffering with a self-righteous attitude. Do you ever judge yourself as being more spiritual than others?

8. Self-righteousness, many times, comes from a lack of knowledge of who we are in Christ. According to Romans 10:1–4, what are Paul's concerns about self-righteousness in the early church?

9. Read Romans 10:4, how does belief in Christ affect the law?

10. Many Christians fail to experience real peace and power in their lives because they don't understand that we have our righteousness in Christ. Until we stop living according to our feelings and learn to stand on who we are in Christ, we will never live in the victory that the Lord purchased for us at Calvary. According to Romans 3:21–28, list what we need to know about our righteousness and justification by faith in Christ.

11. When people are legalistic, they live under the law. They have a list of rules and regulations they must keep in order to feel right with God. They have their list of dos and don'ts they try to live by. The Apostle Paul knew that it would not be an easy transition for the Jews in the early church to go from keeping the law to living under grace. He knew that

they would continue to put confidence in keeping the law. According to Philippians 3:3, in what does Paul tell them to place their confidence?

12. What are the things that Paul warns us to not place our confidence in from Philippians 3:4-6?

13. Notice that all these things are external. How would you relate these things to the church today?

14. What conclusions does Paul make in Philippians 3:8–9 after telling them not to put their confidence in the flesh?

15. Let's look at what Paul's "confidence" list might look like in the church today. As you evaluate this list, examine your own life. Have you placed your confidence in any of these instead of Christ?

☐ Church membership ☐ Baptism ☐ Serving

☐ Certain denomination ☐ Perfect Sunday School attendance

☐ Perfect church attendance ☐ Attending Bible study

☐ Singing in the choir

All these things are good, but we must not put our confidence in them to make us right before God. Our justification and right standing before God comes through faith in Jesus Christ and Him alone.

16. According to Ephesians 2:8–9, how are we saved? In what are we not to boast?

17. When we try to maintain our salvation or righteousness by our own works, what are we doing according to Paul in Galatians 5:4–6?

God wants us to enjoy our freedom in Christ. Yet most of us worry if we are doing enough to make God happy with us, so we enslave ourselves by performing religious activities. God is more interested in having a personal, intimate relationship with us than all the religious activities we try to perform for Him.

Power Challenge

Look over the following list. Circle the actions and attitudes that best describe you. If you recognize any self-righteous and legalistic thinking in your life, confess those areas to God and allow His forgiving power to cleanse you and to heal you.

Self-Righteous/Legalistic (Works of Religious Effort)

- Self-centered
- Try hard (self-effort)
- Obey the rules
- Do a certain number of works in a certain way
- Balance good and bad
- Create own justification system
- Dependence on self
- Receive salvation by works
- Maintain salvation by works
- Believe works will obligate God to respond
- Conformed to set of standards in dress and behavior
- Self-sufficient
- Trying always to keep the law

Righteous in Christ (Works of a Relationship)

- God-centered
- Acknowledge helplessness
- Live by faith
- No accounting or checklist
- God's Word is the standard
- Faith alone justifies
- Dependent on God

- Salvation by faith
- Live by faith
- Have no control over God's will
- Conformed to the image of Christ
- Sufficiency in God
- Freedom in Christ and the Holy Spirit

Our freedom in Christ doesn't mean that we don't have to obey God. If we love God, we will want to obey Him. God gives us the power to obey Him through the Holy Spirit and His grace. God's grace doesn't give us liberty to sin; rather, God's grace gives us power over sin. The good works we do are all as a result of being in a personal relationship with Christ. Remember, we are the workmanship of Christ, created for good works which He planned out for us before the foundation of the earth was set. We need to seek the Lord and find out what good works He has for us to do. When He shows us, we can know that only He can accomplish them through the power of the Holy Spirit and not through the power of the flesh. We can never do the work of the Spirit in the energy of the flesh.

Power Meditation

"There is therefore now no condemnation to those who are in Christ Jesus, who do not walk according to the flesh, but according to the Spirit" (Romans 8:1).

Day 5: The Controlaholic
Power Verse: "Every wise woman builds her house, but the foolish pulls it down with her own hands." (Proverbs 14:1)

The *controlaholic*—otherwise known as a control freak—is another example of someone suffering with the "Martha mentality." When we read the account of Mary and Martha in the Bible, we find that Martha had a need to control what was going on in her life. When Jesus came to her home for dinner, she lost her peace and joy in her need to control everything. She assessed the situation and started giving orders—even to Jesus! In Luke 11:40, Martha told Jesus, "Lord, you do not care that my sister has left me to serve alone." Martha had a plan and an agenda for the evening, and she certainly wasn't going to let Mary or Jesus interfere!

Controlaholics think that everyone should be following their agendas. They continually exercise authority and dominate every activity, every event, and everyone. It is very difficult for controlaholics to trust God because of the fear of losing control. As long as they feel in control of their lives and their circumstances, they think they can have peace. However, that peace doesn't last long because at the first sight of a problem, they try to fix it. Controlaholics not only try to control their own lives but the lives of others. Controlaholics are masters of worry and anxiety. Needless to say, they don't enjoy much peace and joy.

Controlaholics live as though they are general managers of the universe. They are always right and find it difficult to submit to authority. The answer to overcoming being a controlaholic is learning to trust and depend on God in every situation of life.

If you are sick and tired of being a controlaholic, be encouraged. God wants to set you free! We serve a great and powerful God who is in control of the universe and is in control of every detail of our personal lives as well. He is trustworthy, dependable, and faithful.

Let go! And let God!

1. On a scale from 1 to 10, how would you relate your need for control?
2. How does your need to be in control of everything rob you of peace and joy?
3. Check the areas where you have difficulty trusting in God.

☐ Marriage	☐ Finances	☐ Career	☐ Ministry
☐ Health	☐ Future	☐ Children	☐ Guidance
☐ Prayer	☐ Friendships	☐ Death	☐ Peace
☐ Happiness	☐ Making		
☐ Other	changes		

4. Spend a moment to examine the above list and the areas you checked. Ask yourself and God why you have a difficult time trusting Him in those areas. Record your insights.

   This is a personal time between you and God. Don't feel that you have to discuss it in class.

5. Many times we think we can control circumstances because we think we understand what caused them. According to Proverbs 3:5, what are we instructed to do?

6. "Leaning on our own understanding" means to put confidence in our own natural, carnal reasoning. In what ways do you lean upon your own understanding instead of trusting God?

7. According to Proverbs 3:6, what does God promise to do if we acknowledge Him in all of our ways?

8. We don't need to know everything. We have a wonderful promise in Proverbs 3:5–6 that God will direct our paths if we trust Him to do it. How can knowing and applying this truth help set us free from wanting to control everything?

9. How can applying Proverbs 20:24 to our lives relieve stress and tensions?

10. What promises do we have to stand on in Psalm 37:23–24 when we are tempted to try to control the outcome of a particular situation?

11. The controlaholic has a sister named worry. In a prior study, we saw how worry is a sin. Worried and controlling people are simply showing their lack of trust and dependence on God. According to Psalm 127:1–3, how fruitless is it to worry and to try to control our lives?

12. Fill in the blank and personalize the above Scripture. For example, "Unless the Lord builds my ministry...," "Unless the Lord watches over my children...," "Unless the Lord gives me children..."

13. Look up the word *vain* in a dictionary and record your insight.

14. What areas in your life have you been trying to control where you now realize your efforts are fruitless and empty (other than giving you an ulcer)?

15. Psalm 127:1–2 tells us that excessive care about things of this world is vain and fruitless. We can work from morning until late at night, and without God's blessing and sanction on our work, it will never succeed. Read Haggai 1:6. How do we see the fruitlessness of trying to control and worry over our lives?

16. Psalm 127:2 tells us that sleep is a gift from God. When we trust and depend upon God, He promises to give His beloved sleep.

17. Psalm 127:3 tells us that our children are a gift from God. If we are given children, it is because God has given them to us. Read Genesis 30:2 and Genesis 33:4–5. How do these scriptures comfort us concerning having children?

18. How can the following verses help to set us free from being controlaholics?

Psalm 121
Psalm 139:1–7, 16
Psalm 18:30–36
Psalm 125:1–2

Power Challenge

In summary, I can be set free from being a controlaholic because

* God directs my path, and He orders my steps.
* God is in control; therefore, I labor in vain when I try to control.
* God will take care of me, my children, my family.
* God will not allow my foot to be moved.
* God keeps me.
* God neither sleeps nor slumbers.
* God preserves my life from evil.

- God has placed a hedge of protection behind me and before me.
- God has written the number of my days in His book.
- God's ways are perfect.
- God is my shield and my salvation.
- God's right hand upholds me.
- God enlarges my path so that I can't slip.

The Scripture above describes God's character and attributes. We see how powerful and mighty God really is. I want to encourage you as you learn more of God's attributes to implement them into your prayers. Thank God that He will direct your path, and He will sustain you and preserve you from evil. Implement these truths about God as you pray for your family and loved ones.

Power Meditation

> "Cast your burden on the Lord,
> and He shall sustain you;
> He shall never permit
> the righteous to be moved" (Psalm 55:22).

Chapter 8
Do You Suffer with ITD (Impaired Thinking Disorder)?

Power Verse: "Out of the same mouth proceed blessing and cursing. My brethren, these things ought not to be so. Does a spring send forth fresh water and bitter from the same opening?" (James 3:10–11)

Impaired thinking for the Christian is thinking that handicaps and disables us from running our Christian race victoriously. Renewing of the mind is paramount for every born-again believer. To just get saved and be on your way to heaven is not what God intended for His children. To be impaired is to cause to diminish, as in strength, value, and quality. God wants our lives to be lived at a higher quality level; instead, many of us settle for a lower quality of life because we aren't daily renewing our minds by the Word of God. When the church continues to think like the world, our values become impaired, and we lose our strength and ability to influence the world for Jesus Christ. Impaired thinking in a Christian's life is manifested by inconsistent behavior, doublemindedness, fear, negative thinking, and negative speech. James tells us that it is inconsistent for us to praise and bless God one minute and curse our neighbor in our next breath. When our tongue blesses the Father and turns around and curses man, who has been made in God's image, this evidences a heart that is in need of spiritual medicine. A tongue that is inconsistent is evidence that there is contamination and pollution in the wellspring of our heart. It is not the tongue that is defiled but the heart. In Matthew 15:18, Jesus said that those things which proceed out of the mouth come forth from the heart, and they defile the man. Without a doubt, we can say that we are all guilty of the inconsistency that James is talking about. Nonetheless, the Lord is not honored by this kind of behavior, and He has given us the power to rise to a higher level and a higher quality of life—one that is free of inconsistency, doublemindedness, and fear.

We have all been exposed to the common carriers of ITD: the devil, the flesh, and the world. When impaired thinking goes untreated long enough, it can lead to unhealthy and destructive lifestyles like those prevalent in our world today. One way to diagnose ITD is to listen to your own words. Jesus said that out of the abundance of the heart, the mouth speaks. If we want to know what is in our hearts, we just have to listen to what comes out of our mouths. The prescription for ITD is daily megadoses of God's Word. Deuteronomy 8:3 says that man does not live by bread alone but by every word that proceeds from the mouth of God.

Day 1: Are You Suffering from a Double Mind?

Power Verse: "And Elijah came to all the people, and said, 'How long will you falter between two opinions? If the Lord is God, follow Him; but if Baal, then follow him.'" (1 Kings 18:21)

Doubt is a powerful tool used by the enemy to attack our faith. To doubt, or to be doubleminded, is trying to walk with two minds or to stand in two ways. It implies uncertainty as to which way to take, being anxious, with a distracted mind, wavering between hope and fear. Doubt will cause us to waver between two opinions. God fills our hearts with faith, but the devil wants to destroy our faith by getting us to doubt.

Doubt comes in the form of thoughts that are in opposition to God's plans for our lives. This is why it is so important for us to know the Word of God so that we will recognize when the devil is lying to us. Doubting is a choice, just as standing in faith is a choice. We can either keep our eyes on the circumstances and believe what we see with our natural eyes, or we can choose to believe God, who already knows about our circumstances and has them under control.

Doubt leads to discouragement, depression, and despair. If you are a doubting Thomas, be encouraged; God wants to set you free from a double mind.

1. Are you a habitual doubter or just an occasional doubter?
2. What kinds of doubts do you experience that interfere with your ability to trust God?
3. Read Matthew 14:25–32. Where was Jesus, and where were His disciples?
4. Describe the emotions the disciples felt when they saw Jesus walking on the water. What was Jesus's response to them?
5. Walking on water is not a natural act but a supernatural act. No one had ever seen another person walk on water before. Do you welcome the supernatural move of God in your life, or are you troubled and fearful when God seems to want to do something different than you expected?
6. In Matthew 14:28–29, Peter asked Jesus to command him to walk on the water. Jesus said, "Come." What was Peter's response to Jesus's command in verse 29?
7. It took faith for Peter to believe he could walk on the water. Did Peter's faith start when he was getting out of the boat or when he was on the water?
8. According to Matthew 14:30–31, what destroyed Peter's faith?
9. When we get our eyes off Jesus and begin to focus on our circumstances or conditions, it can cause us to begin to doubt and waver between two opinions. We begin to waver between hope and fear. We will either believe what we see in the natural and doubt, or faith will rise up inside us and we will trust in God. Do you have circumstances in your own life right now that are causing you to waver between two opinions?
10. The greatest demonstration of Peter's faith was when he got out of the boat. Peter had already decided that nothing was impossible for Jesus, and if Jesus said to come, then

he could walk on water. So many times when God calls us into the deep waters of change, we want to stay in our comfort boats and are unwilling to get out of them because we prefer to walk in familiarity rather than walk by faith. If God called you to do something totally new and different, would you be willing to get out of your comfort boat and step out in faith to walk on the deep waters of unfamiliar territory?

11. One of the most important things we need is Godly wisdom as we face the challenges of life. According to James 1:5–6, how does God give wisdom to us and on what basis are we to ask God for wisdom?

12. How does James 1:6 describe the man who doubts?

13. Read James 1:7–8, what is the result of a man who habitually doubts?

14. In your own words, what do you think it means to ask God in faith with no doubting? Do you see a choice that has to be made concerning faith and doubt?

15. Read Hebrews 11:1 and, in your own words, explain what faith is.

16. As born-again believers, we have been saved and justified by faith in the Lord Jesus Christ. How does Romans 1:17 say that the just are to live?

We must make a choice to walk in faith with no doubting. Doubt is an enemy to our faith, and it will keep us from receiving all the good things God has for us. According to the following verses, what choices must we make about walking by faith and not doubting?

2 Corinthians 5:7
Hebrews 11:6
Hebrews 10:23

17. Throughout the gospels, Jesus talks about faith. He always mentioned the size of a person's faith as being no faith, little faith, or great faith. In the following verses, note the

size of the person's faith, and what his or her faith accomplished. What do doubt and unbelief do to our faith?

Matthew 17:17–20
Matthew 21:21–22
Mark 5:34
Luke 7:1–10
Luke 17:11–19
Luke 18:35–43

Our faith is only as good as its object. We can't put faith in faith itself because there would be no power. When the object of our faith is God Almighty, then it is powerful faith because He is a powerful God. Our faith grows as we meditate on the attributes of God. Romans 10:17 says that faith comes by hearing and hearing by the Word of God. The more we know the Word of God and the God of the Word, the more our faith will grow. As we step out in faith, believing God to meet our needs, believing and not doubting, our faith muscles get stronger and stronger. We must make a choice every day to walk by faith and not doubt.

18. Finally, Ephesians 6:13–18 tells us to put on the full armor of God so that we will be able to withstand in the evil day. Part of the armor is the shield of faith, which will quench the darts of doubt from the evil one. From today's lesson, list all the ways you can appropriate the shield of faith and quench the fiery darts of doubt every day.

19. How has God spoken to you today?

Power Challenge

When we doubt, we must not waver in our faith but have full assurance that what God has promised, He is able to perform (Romans 4:21). Faith is believing and trusting in God, in spite of my feelings or my circumstances. Remember that doubt will shut down our faith and paralyze us in our Christian walk. Without faith, it is impossible to please God. When we go to God, we must not doubt but believe that He is God, and He promises to reward us when we diligently seek Him. Jesus said that even if our faith was as small as a mustard seed, that we have mountain-moving faith if we believe in our hearts and don't doubt. Jesus said that nothing shall be impossible for the one who believes in Him and does not doubt. When the devil tries to shoot darts of doubt into your mind, reject them in the name of Jesus and promptly bring those doubting thoughts captive to the obedience of Christ. Praise God and thank Him for His promises. Choose from this day forward that you are not going to doubt and do without, but that you are going to believe and receive.

Power Meditation

> "Being confident of this very thing, that He who has begun a good work in you will complete it until the day of Jesus Christ" (Philippians 1:6).

Day 2: Fear Not
Power Verse: "For I, the Lord your God, will hold your right hand, saying to you, 'Fear not, I will help you.'" (Isaiah 41:13)

We live in a world today that makes people feel fearful. To experience fear is to be afraid. It is a feeling of fright, dread, terror, panic, and trepidation. Fear is the inclination to feel anxiety or apprehension in the presence of danger. The phrase *fear not* is used in the Bible several hundred times. God knew that His people would experience fear. In many of the same passages, God also says "to fear not but to be strong and of good courage." God wants to fill our hearts with courage and faith, but the devil wants to fill our minds and hearts with fear so that we will fail to become the overcomers intended by God. The Greek word for fear is *phobos*, the same word from which we get the word phobia. Fear is a phobia and a demonic spirit sent from the enemy to destroy our faith. We can experience fear of the future, fear of failure, fear over finances, fear of death or danger. We can even experience fear and dread of God when we feel

He is displeased with us. Proverbs 1:7 says that the fear of the Lord is the beginning of knowledge. This type of fear is not a frightful, dreading kind of fear but an awesome reverence for who God is. It is healthy for every child of God to have reverence for God because He is mighty, powerful, and all-knowing, in control over the affairs of this world. Fear can be a good emotion when it promotes good health. You would not go out and lie down in the middle of the road because of the fear of being run over and killed. You wouldn't drive 120 mph down a major freeway because of the fear of losing control of your vehicle and crashing.

The type of fear we will be evaluating today is the spirit of fear sent by Satan to paralyze our minds from trusting God and moving forward in our faith. God has given us the power to defeat fear when we put on the shield of faith, use the sword of the Spirit (the Word), and prevail through the power of prayer. Fear is Satan's source of power just as faith is God's source of power. Let's put on our spiritual armor and put away that spirit of fear.

1. On a scale of 1–10, rate fear in your life in the following areas:

   Fear of failure
   Fear of the future
   Fear over finances
   Fear of sickness and disease
   Fear of danger
   Fear of death
   Other

2. According to Romans 8:2, what two spiritual principles are at work in our world?

3. Read Genesis 3:6–10. What was the first emotion that Adam experienced after he sinned in the garden in verse 10?

   When Adam bowed his knee to Satan, he put the law of sin and death into motion. He died spiritually and began to die physically as well. The knowledge of the law of sin and death produces fear, and we see this in Adam's statement to God in the garden, that he was afraid and tried to hide from God.

4. When you commit a sin, do you become fearful of God and try to hide your sin, or do you confess your sin to God, get cleansed, and experience His forgiveness and receive restoration to fellowship with Him?

5. In Romans 8:2, we see the two spiritual laws, the law of the spirit of life and the law of sin and death. Jesus offered Himself as the supreme sacrifice to purchase our freedom from the law of sin and death. According to Hebrews 2:14–15, what two things did Jesus do for us at Calvary?

6. Read Romans 8:15, what two spirits are contrasted in this passage, and how do each work in the life of a believer?

7. Fear is a spiritual force just as faith is a spiritual force. According to 2 Timothy 1:7, what does God say about fear and what are the characteristics of the Spirit that God has given us?

8. Fear activates Satan's power in the same way that faith activates God's power. Fear is totally destructive and cripples our minds. Read 1 John 4:18 and record your insights on what fear produces in our lives and what is our answer in casting fear out of our lives.

    Fear is a satanic force that works against us. Faith is a creative force that God uses to build and uplift. Fear tears us down and destroys. Whenever we are walking by faith, our lives will always benefit from it. Whenever fear is in operation, we will be subject to bondage and torment. God's perfect love will cast out fear.

9. We may know that God loves us but still have fear. If we still fear, it is because we need to grow in our understanding of how much God really loves us. Do you habitually walk in the truth that God loves you fully, totally, and completely?

10. We walk in God's love as we walk keeping His Word in our hearts, minds, and mouths. When we stand on God's Word in every situation of life, we will overcome fear. According to 1 John 4:4, why can we overcome?

Faith power is not produced in our heads but in our hearts. It is produced by the Word of God being fed into our spirits. If we operate in fear and feed fear down into our spirits, we will never produce the kind of faith power it takes to rule over the circumstances of this life. God wants us to walk believing and meditating on His Word and not believing and meditating on the problem. "For we walk by faith, not by sight" (2 Corinthians 5:7).

11. According to the following Scriptures, write your insights on how we can get free from fear.

Psalm 118:6
Joshua 1:9
1 Chronicles 28:20
Isaiah 43:1–2
Romans 8:31, 37–39

Faith comes by hearing the Word of God and acting upon it. Fear comes by hearing the word of the world (Satan's lies) and acting on it. The devil's weapon against us is fear. Our most powerful weapon against him is the Word of God. Learn to use the weapon of the Word to combat Satan's lies by believing, praying, and speaking the Word of God in every situation.

12. We can walk in faith and not in fear, knowing that we have angelic protection. What insights can you gain about this wonderful truth from the following Scriptures?

Psalm 91:9–13
Psalm 103:20
2 Kings 6:15–17

13. We should pray about everything and fear nothing. When we pray, we release our faith to work in our circumstances. According to 1 Thessalonians 5:17 and Matthew 26:41, how should we pray?

14. What do you think it means to pray unceasingly, and what types of things do you think we need to be watchful for as we pray?

15. What have you learned from God's Word today that has encouraged you to reset your mindset from fear to faith?

Power Challenge

Fear is fed through our minds into our spirits. Fear is not natural for the believer; it comes from the outside. In Matthew 12:34, Jesus said that out of the abundance of the heart, the mouth speaks. We get fear into our spirits by speaking it. We need to stop practicing fear by using it in our daily conversation. Instead, we need to develop the habit of speaking the Word of God. Remember that the weapons of our warfare are not carnal but mighty in God to the pulling down of strongholds (2 Corinthians 10:4–5). When fear comes on the scene, bring that thought into captivity to the obedience of Christ. Fear will impair our thinking and weaken our faith. Make a decision today to refuse fear in Jesus's name and decide not to act upon or practice fear in any way.

Power Meditation

"And the Lord, He is the One who goes before you. He will be with you; He will not leave you nor forsake you; do not fear nor be dismayed" (Deuteronomy 31:8).

Day 3: Inconsistent Thinking and Behavior
Power Verse: "But above all, my brethren, do not swear, either by heaven or by earth or with any other oath. But let your 'Yes' be 'Yes,' and your 'No,' 'No,' lest you fall into judgment." (James 5:12)

Inconsistent thinking impairs us from living the transformed life that God desires for His children. Inconsistent thinking will lead to erratic behavior. When we are inconsistent, there are discrepancies between what we say and what we do. We cannot walk in agreement and harmony between ourselves and others and be inconsistent at the same time. Inconsistent thinking and behavior directly results when a Christian isn't experiencing transformation but is allowing himself or herself to be conformed to the world's way of thinking. We see so many inconsistencies in the world, and if the world is shaping our values more than is the Word of God, our lives will have inconsistencies as well. People who are inconsistent are usually unpredictable, likely to have a change of mind, fickle and faithless. We will develop more consistent thinking and behavior as we learn the importance of walking the Spirit-filled and Spirit-led life. Galatians 5:17 says that the flesh lusts against the Spirit and the Spirit against the flesh so that you do not do the things you wish. God desires that we develop consistent patterns of thinking and behavior and have lifestyles that are reliable and steady. God wants His children to reflect His character and personality upon this earth. There are no inconsistencies in God. He always remains constant, faithful, and sure. The Word of God says in Hebrews 13:8 that He is the same today, yesterday, and forever. The way we overcome inconsistent thinking and behavior is to first realize the problem exists in our own lives, confess it to God and, by the power of the Holy Spirit, determine to become a faithful child of God.

1. Check the areas where you want to become more consistent. This is not an exhaustive list, so you may have other areas not mentioned with which you want to deal.

   ☐ Sending thank you cards or notes of encouragement
   ☐ Getting places on time
   ☐ Praying
   ☐ Disciplining my children
   ☐ Reading the Bible
   ☐ Encouraging others
   ☐ Praising my husband or wife
   ☐ Exercise

☐   Scripture meditation
☐   Exercising discipline in areas of weakness
☐   Serving God with my gifts
☐   Keeping commitments
☐   Thought life
☐   What I say vs. what I do
☐   Emotions
☐   Other

2.   What inconsistency is James showing us in James 3:8–12, and how does it manifest itself?

3.   What illustrations does James use to get his readers to understand his point about being inconsistent?

4.   How about you? Do you find times when you praise and bless the Lord in the morning, only to find yourself cursing at your friends and loved ones by noon time? Inconsistent thinking is evidenced in our speech. When we see inconsistency in our behavior, it is because we are not lining up our thinking with the Word of God on a consistent basis. If we want to change those old carnal thinking patterns, we must let the Word of God to saturate our minds that our conversations with others will reflect the mind of Christ.

5.   What type of conduct and character should we be demonstrating in our lives, according to James 3:13?

6.   In the above verse of Scripture in James, how do you think James is trying to relate wisdom and understanding to inconsistent speech?

7.   Read Matthew 26:32–35, 69–75. How was Peter inconsistent in these passages?

8.   Do you think the pressure of the moment caused Peter to be inconsistent, or do you think this was a problem he already had?

9.   Read Matthew 26:75. How do you think Peter felt when he heard the rooster crow three times and then remembered what Jesus had said to him?

Many times, inconsistent thinking will lead us to deny the Lord, just as Peter did. Denial can be a very subtle thing to detect in our own lives. We don't have to deny we know Jesus, like Peter did, to be guilty of denying the Lord. We deny the Lord when we don't consistently spend time in His Word. We deny the Lord when we don't make prayer a priority every day. We deny the Lord when we don't use our spiritual gifts to serve Him and others. We deny the Lord when we fail to witness to the lost and don't take care of the poor and homeless.

10. What inconsistencies in your life are leading you to deny the Lord?

11. Peter denied Jesus three times, right before He went to the cross. In John 21, we have the account of Jesus, after His resurrection, meeting with His disciples at the sea and having breakfast with them. In John 21:14–19, what does Jesus's conversation with Peter reveal to us about Jesus's personality and attributes?

12. We have seen how Jesus sought out Peter and restored him after he denied Jesus three times. Jesus called Peter to follow Him and to feed His sheep. How does Peter respond to Jesus's call in John 21:20–22?

13. Who or what are you looking at that keeps you from faithfully following the Lord?

14. Look up the definition of the following words:

Faithful
Steward

15. How does inconsistent thinking and behavior keep you from being a faithful steward?

16. God has called us to be faithful stewards over everything He has entrusted into our hands while we are on this earth. We are to be faithful stewards of our time, talents, gifts, and resources. What important principles can we learn about stewardship from Matthew 25:14–29 and Luke 16:10?

17. From James, we have seen that inconsistent thinking manifests itself in our words. The Lord wants us to be faithful stewards of our words because our words ultimately lead to our deeds. In Matthew 12:36–37, what is Jesus's warning concerning our words?

18. How do the following verses encourage us to be faithfully consistent in honoring our commitments?

   2 Corinthians 1:17–20
   James 5:12

19. In light of what we have studied today, have you been able to identify areas of inconsistency? If so, how has God's Word challenged you to change?

Power Challenge

If the Holy Spirit has helped you recognize areas in your life that are inconsistent, confess those areas to your Heavenly Father (1 John 1:9). Ask the Lord to give you determination through the power of the Holy Spirit to press on to victory. Like Daniel, purpose in your heart to become consistent, reliable, and steadfast in your walk with the Lord (Daniel 1:8). Tell the Lord it is your desire to be found faithful by Him and that one day you want to hear the words, "Well done, good and faithful servant. You were faithful over a few things; I will make you faithful over many things. Enter into the joy of the Lord."

Power Meditation

   "And whatever you do in word or deed, do all in
   the name of the Lord Jesus, giving thanks to God
   the Father through Him" (Colossians 3:17).

Day 4: Controlling the Tongue
Power Verse: "Whoever guards his mouth and tongue keeps his soul from troubles." (Proverbs 21:23)

Jesus said in Matthew 12:34 that out of the abundance of the heart, the mouth speaks. Our mouth gives expression to what we think, feel, and desire. This is one important reason why every believer should daily be in a process of renewing our minds to think like God thinks. Without renewing of the mind, our thinking will be carnal, natural, and fleshly, instead of godly. Our words will reflect whether we are fleshly or spiritual. Our mouths can either be a mouthpiece for God or a mouthpiece for the devil. We can speak words that build up, or we can speak words that tear down. Many of the problems that Christians have are mostly due to the negative way we speak. If we were to tape record everything we say in a period of a week, we would be shocked. At the same time, we would understand why we have some of the problems we have. Do you speak negative words or positive words? Many Christians get uptight when they are told to think positive, as if being positive associates them with a cult. Jesus never spoke negatively, and in Ephesians 5:1, we are told to imitate God as beloved children. When we line up our thinking and our words with the Word of God and talk about our situation the way Jesus would talk about it, we will open ourselves up to experience the mighty, miracle-working power of God in our lives. Negative, destructive, and critical words impair our spiritual growth and effectiveness for the Lord. I encourage you to purpose in your heart to become a powerful mouthpiece for God.

1. List the negative or ungodly words or statements you often speak and want to overcome.
2. Read James 3: 1 - 8. In this passage, James uses five illustrations to reveal the power of our tongues. As we look at each one, what do you think his point is as it relates to the power of the tongue? Write down your insights.

Verse 3 — The bit or bridle
Verse 4 — The rudder
Verse 5 — The forest fire
Verse 7 — The animals
Verse 8 — Deadly poison

Our tongues have the power to direct and power to destroy. In using the illustration of the bit and the rudder, James presented two things that are physically small yet exercise great power, just like the tongue. A small bit enables a rider to control a great horse, and a small rudder enables a pilot to steer a huge ship. Both the bit and the rudder must overcome contrary forces. The wild nature of the horse could unseat the rider, and the winds and currents of the sea could drive a ship off its course. The human tongue also must overcome the contrary forces of the old fleshly nature, which wants to control us and make us sin. Our tongues have the power to direct our lives and the lives of others. When we bring our tongues under the control of the Holy Spirit, He helps us to direct the lives of others in the right way. James uses fire, animals, and poison to help us see how the tongue has the power to destroy lives. Our words can start fires and heat things up. A hot head and a hot heart can lead to heated words that we will later regret. Our tongue can set the course of our destiny on fire, and lives are destroyed in the process. Wild animals are capable of doing great damage, even killing. Some animals are poisonous, just as some tongues are poisonous, and spread the poison. Jesus can't be Lord of our lives until He is Lord of our lips.

3. Have you ever had times when something you said to a friend, business associate, or loved one got out of control?

4. James 3:8 says a man's tongue is full of unruly evil and deadly poison, and a man can't tame it. If man can't tame his tongue, how do you think it would be possible to control your tongue?

5. Have you brought your mouth and tongue under the control of the Holy Spirit?

6. How do John 6:63 and Galatians 6:8 relate to each other as to the contrast between the Spirit and the flesh and our words?

7. Are the words you are sowing in your life and the lives of others producing peace and harmony or disagreement and discord?

8. According to Proverbs 18:20–21, what do our words have the power to produce in our lives?

9. In your own words, how do you think we are satisfied by the fruit of our lips?

    Our words have the power to produce the fruit of life or the fruit of death. Words are like seeds that we sow every day. We will either be satisfied from the fruit of life that we have sown in our own lives and in the lives of others, or we will have dissatisfied lives as a result of the fruit of death that we have sown into our lives and the lives of others.

10. Ask yourself the following questions concerning your words. Have I been sowing

    Words of encouragement or words of discouragement?
    Words of praise or words of criticism?
    Words of joy or words of sadness?
    Words of peace or words of strife?
    Words of faith or words of fear?
    Words of comfort or words of dread?
    Words of acceptance or words of condemnation?
    Words of truth or words of deception?
    Words of life or words of death?

11. What kind of words do you want to sow into the lives of your children, spouse, and friends that you are not presently sowing?

12. Read Ephesians 4:29–32. What does Paul exhort us to do concerning our manner of speaking?

13. What does corrupt, bitter, and angry speech do to God, according to Ephesians 4:30?

14. Instead of speaking critically of others, what are we exhorted to do according to Ephesians 4:32?

15. As a life habit, are you speaking words to others that edify and impart grace, or are you speaking words that impart judgment?

    God shows abundant grace and mercy toward us, and He wants us to be imitators of Him and show grace and mercy to others, especially to the household of faith. It pleases God when we speak the right things to each other. At the same time, it displeases Him when we speak critical, faultfinding, bitter, and angry words to each other. Our words can grieve the Holy Spirit, who lives inside us. Perhaps, some of the grief we experience in our own lives is due to our grieving the Holy Spirit by speaking words that tear down and destroy.

16. Once we let our tongues get out of control, it seems as though everything gets out of control. According to James 1:19, what choices do we need to make concerning our words?

17. According to James 1:20, when we don't control our tongues and we speak angry words to each other, what is not being produced in our lives?

18. Our Power Verse for the day, Proverbs 21:23, says that whoever guards his mouth and tongue keeps his soul from trouble. This means we could avoid a lot of trouble in our lives if we would just learn to control our tongues. How can the following verses encourage us to bring our tongues under the control of the Holy Spirit?

    1 Peter 3:9–12
    Matthew 15:11
    Psalm 19:14
    Proverbs 15:1–4
    Proverbs 4:23–24

19. How do we see the progression of our words leading to our deeds in Proverbs 4:23–27?

20. What has the Holy Spirit said to you today about your tongue?

166

Power Challenge

Give God your tongue and your heart each day, and ask Him to use you to be a blessing to others. Isaiah 50:4 says, "The Lord God has given me the tongue of the learned, that I should know how to speak a word in season to him who is weary... He awakens my ear to hear as the learned." If you and I are going to be mighty mouthpieces for the Lord and speak words that are a delight to His ears, then we must meet with the Lord each day and learn from Him. We must get our spiritual roots deep into His Word. I challenge you to pray, meditate on His Word, and allow the Holy Spirit to fill your heart with His love and truth. Begin today to use the following phrases, which will transform your life:

> "Please."
> "Thank you."
> "I'm sorry."
> "I love you."
> "I'm praying for you."

When you and I speak these encouraging words to others, it lets them know we really care enough about them to meet them at the throne of grace.

Power Meditation

> "Set a guard, O Lord, over my mouth; Keep watch over the door of my lips" (Psalm 141:3).

Day 5: Mastering My Mouth

Power Verse: "If anyone among *you* thinks he is religious and does not bridle his tongue but deceives his own heart, this one's religion is useless." (James *1:26*)

Yesterday, we dealt with the importance of controlling the tongue. The tongue is the world's smallest but largest troublemaker and deserves another day of looking into God's Word to see what He has to say about our tongues and how to master our mouths. In James, we learned that the tongue has the power to direct, destroy, and do great damage. It appears that the Christians to whom James was writing were having real problems with their tongues. The power of speech is one of the greatest powers and privileges given to us by God. We can use our mouths to praise God, pray to God, preach the Word, and lead the lost to Christ.

But with that same tongue, we can tell lies that could ruin a person's reputation and crush his soul. As Christians, we have an opportunity and a privilege to influence others with our words and accomplish great tasks, but many take this privilege for granted. James 3:2 says, "We all stumble in many things. If anyone does not stumble in word, he is a perfect man, able also to bridle the whole body." James is saying that mastering our mouths gives evidence as to how spiritually mature we are. When James uses the word *perfect*, he does not mean that the person has reached sinless perfection, but that he is complete, fully grown, and mature in his faith. From this verse, we also see that if we have the ability to bridle our own tongues, we also have the ability to bridle our whole bodies. In other words, if we can learn to master our mouths, we will be able to master our lives as well.

James tells us that the tongue is full of deadly poison, and no man can tame it. If we want to master our mouths, we must choose to let the Master above become the master of our mouths. We must start listening to our words and begin cooperating with the Holy Spirit, making our words accountable to God. Without God, we can't change anything, but when we agree with Him and His Word, all things are possible, even mastering our mouths. Today's Power Verse says that if we don't bridle our tongues, we are deceiving our hearts, and our religion is worthless. Let's take a look into God's Word and into our lives to discover whether we have a useless or a useful religion.

1. What areas of speech is God showing you that you need to master?
2. Read today's Power Verse again. Practically speaking, how do you think a bridled tongue reveals the quality and value of one's religion?

3. How do you think we can be deceived in our hearts by not having a bridled tongue?

4. James 1:19 says that we are to be quick to hear, slow to speak, and slow to anger. Usually speaking, do you think about what you say before you say it, or do you just speak freely whatever and whenever you feel like speaking?

5. According to Isaiah 50:4, how is a child of God to speak and why?

6. According to this verse, what is the link to you and I becoming learned of tongue?

God wants His people to speak with a heavenly language. Our hearts and minds should be so saturated with the Word of God that it flows from our lips like a heavenly language. We need to get our thinking and our words lined up and in agreement with the Word of God. Since our words have tremendous power in them, we need to be careful which ones we speak. Our words have the power to affect our spiritual, emotional, and physical health, as well as our future. The most natural way for the flesh to think is to dwell on the negative side of life. Let's purpose in our hearts to be people led by the Spirit of God and walking and talking the life of faith.

7. Our words are power containers. Natural, fleshly, carnal words contain power to destroy and damage lives. On the other hand, faith-filled words that are in agreement with the Word of God contain enough power to move mountains, according to Jesus's words in Matthew 17:20. We can also see how powerful the Word of God is in Genesis 1. God created the heaven and the earth, life and all its elements by simply speaking the Word. We can read in the first chapter of Genesis, over and over, "God said...and it was so." According to Hebrews 4:12, how is the Word of God described?

8. Are your conversations with others filled with the Word of God or the cares and concerns of this world?

9. The devil loves for us to believe his lies because he knows if we believe his lies instead of God's Word, pretty soon we

will begin talking about the problem and walking by our feelings and not our faith. Read Matthew 4:1–11. How did Jesus overcome the lies of the devil as He was tempted in the wilderness?

10. What was the result of Jesus speaking the Word of God to the devil in Matthew 4:11?

11. How does Jesus's example show us the importance of knowing the Word of God and speaking the Word of God in the midst of temptations?

12. Many times it seems our mouths have minds of their own.
    However, the root source of our words is our thoughts. If Satan offers us a thought like, "What's the use? I might as well give up," pretty soon our mouths will be engaged in verbalizing that thought. What are we instructed to do with our thoughts, according to 2 Corinthians 10:5?

13. If we want to think thoughts and speak words that will bear good fruit, what does Philippians 4: 8 instruct us to think about?

14. Our Power Verse today, James 1:26, says that if we want useful religion, we must master our mouths by learning to bridle our tongues. The Holy Spirit is the only bridle powerful enough to master our mouths. What areas has God shown you today that the Holy Spirit needs to master?

Power Challenge

Our fallen nature gravitates toward the wrong things. It wants to find fault with others and ourselves. It wants to magnify the problems. Our born-again nature wants to do good and magnify God. Either way, we have a choice. Every day we have the opportunity to speak a good report or an evil report. Choose today to allow the Holy Spirit to bridle your tongue. A horse either follows the pull of the bridle, which controls his mouth, or he experiences great pain. The same is true for us in our relationship with the Holy Spirit. He is our bridle and wants to control the reins of our life. If we choose to follow His promptings, He will lead us to the right places, and we will avoid a lot of pain. Start praying Psalm 141:3, "Set a guard, O Lord, over my mouth; keep watch over the door of my lips," and God will help you to master your mouth.

Power Meditation

"This Book of the Law shall not depart from your mouth, but you shall meditate in it day and night, that you may observe to do according to all that is written in it. For then you will make your way prosperous, and then you will have good success" (Joshua 1:8).

Chapter 9
A Victor Armed and Dangerous

Power Verse: "Do not be afraid nor dismayed because of this great multitude, for the battle is not yours but God's." (2 Chronicles 20:15)

Bless you, beloved child of God. You have persevered over these last eight weeks, and you have run the race, fought the good fight, and gloriously made it to the finish line. Maybe you don't think of yourself as armed and dangerous but you are. You have learned some very important principles over the past few weeks, such as found in Proverbs 23:7, that right thinking is vital for the Christian "for as he thinks in his heart, so is he." Our minds need to be renewed to think like God wants us to think. Our natural thinking and reasoning tend to gravitate toward the negative side of life, so Romans 12:2 tells us, "Do not be conformed to this world but be transformed by the renewing of your mind..." We have also learned that our minds are Satan's battlefield and that there is a spiritual battle being waged between the flesh and the spirit (Galatians 5:17, 2 Corinthians 10:3–5). We have looked at many different types of attitudes and directions that are a direct result of wrong thinking patterns. Over and over, we have seen that so much of the way we think, speak, and act is a result of the choices we make.

In light of what we have learned over the past eight weeks, we must realize that God has begun a work in us and will give us the power we need to continue to press on to victory in every area. As we end this study, we will look at how we can unleash God's overcoming power in our lives—power to overcome in every situation and circumstance of life. While the devil would like to see us perceive ourselves as defeated, God wants us to see ourselves as overcoming victors, armed and dangerous, because as 2 Chronicles 10:15 says, "The battle is not yours but God's." When we grasp the truth that our mighty, powerful, and loving God goes before us to fight our battles, we will learn to rest in Him and quit wearing ourselves out, trying to fight and win our own battles. This week, we will come into a greater understanding of how armed and dangerous we are as we learn to unleash the power of praise in our lives.

Day 1: Praise: An Act of the Will

Power Verse: *"I will praise You, O Lord, with my whole heart; I will tell of all Your marvelous works. I will be glad and rejoice in You; I will sing praise to Your name, O Most High." (Psalm 9:1–2)*

Praise is an act of worship absent in the lives of many of God's children. We know from the Word of God that He delights in our praises, and Psalm 22:3 says that God inhabits the praises of His people. When we praise God, His power and presence are near. He actually indwells, inhabits, or resides in our praises. Praise is not a magic formula for success but should be the habit of every child of God. We don't praise God for what we want from Him but for who He is. We praise Him because He is our loving Creator, who is infinite in power, wisdom, and strength. He alone is God, and there is no other like Him. He has no beginning and no end. We should praise God because we are His finite creatures, who have a beginning and an end, and our days and our times are in His hands. He is also our loving Savior, who has redeemed us from His wrath to come. When we praise God, something supernatural begins to happen in our lives. His power will flow into our situation, and we will soon notice a change in or around us. Nothing may change in our situation or circumstances, but God will give us peace and joy in the midst of them. Praise is not a bargaining position with God; we are not to praise Him so He will bless us. Instead, to praise God is to delight ourselves in Him. The psalmist wrote, "Delight yourself also in the Lord, and He shall give you the desires of your heart" (Psalm 37:4). If we look at the order in this verse, we see that we are first to delight ourselves in the Lord, then He will give us the desires of our heart. When we really learn to delight ourselves in God, everything else will become of secondary importance to us. As we close, it is my desire that through this last chapter, you will begin to see God's power in a fresh new way and that it will encourage you to make praising our Awesome God a priority and a habit of your life like never before. Remember the key passage for this study, Romans 12:1–2. God desires that we not be conformed to this world's way of thinking, but that we be transformed by the renewing of our minds. A renewed mind will be evidenced in a life that gives praise and thanks to God. As that praise goes up to God, He will transform us in the process.

1. How would you rate your praise and worship time with the Lord in your own personal time with Him?

2. Do you praise and thank God often, seldom, or rarely?

3. Do you ever sing songs to the Lord?

4. Read today's Power Verse. In your own words, describe King David's heart toward praising God.

5. According to Psalm 7:17 and Psalm 9:1–2, does praising God involve an act of our will or should we only praise God when we feel like it?

6. When we praise God, we are praising Him for who He is and all that He has done, not only in our personal lives but for all that He has done in creation. Read Psalm 33 and list the ways David rejoices in the Lord as well as the things for which David praises God.

7. In Psalm 42:11 and Psalm 43:5, the psalmist says he feels downcast. Today, we would call that depression. How does he deal with his downcast soul?

   When we experience times of depression, that is when we need to go to the Lord and begin to praise Him. Could it be possible that this is where our true deliverance lies? Praise takes our eyes off ourselves and focuses them on the goodness and greatness of God. God's power is released into our lives as we praise Him, and His power lifts our countenance.

8. Describe the times you have been depressed or discouraged and yet you chose to praise God and then experienced His power and presence lift you up out of the pit.

   The Bible tells us David was a man after God's own heart. He was also a man who failed God miserably many times, yet God used and blessed him. One of the reasons God blessed David so abundantly was because he chose to rejoice and praise God no matter what his circumstances were. David's hope and trust were always in God.

9. According to Psalm 63:3–8, what did David know about God that caused him to praise God? What does verse 5 say was the result of David's praise?

10. Worshipping the Lord is the act by which we acknowledge His worth. God is worthy of our praise. List all the declarations made by the psalmist in Psalm 66:1–9 that tell how worthy our God is to be praised.

    In Psalm 50:23, God says that when we praise Him, we glorify Him and that He delights in the praises of His people. According to Revelation 4:8–11, God so desires to be praised that the seraphim stand at His throne worshipping Him day and night, saying "Holy, holy, holy, Lord God Almighty, Who was and is and is to come." Here on earth, God is getting us ready to stand in His presence one day in glory and rejoice exceedingly before His throne.

11. Read Psalm 100. Are you able to make a joyful shout to the Lord and come into His presence with singing? If not, why?

12. How has the Holy Spirit encouraged you today to incorporate praise into your prayer and worship time with Him?

Power Challenge

Praise will draw us into the presence of God and ignite our faith. Praise will fan the flames of our smoldering love into a flaming love for God. Praise will expel the powers of darkness, tear down obstacles, and cause the devil to run. Look up to heaven and praise your mighty Redeemer. Praise Him for His love and faithfulness; praise Him for His power and His goodness. He is worthy of all praise. *Praise the Lord!*

Power Meditation

> "Praise the Lord! For it is good to sing praises to our God; for it is pleasant, and praise is beautiful" (Psalm 147:1).

Day 2: Prayer: Faith in Action

Power Verse: "O Lord God of our fathers, are You not God in heaven, and do You not rule over all the kingdoms of the nations, and in Your hand is there not power and might, so that no one is able to withstand You?" (2 Chronicles 20:6)

1. Jehoshaphat, king of Judah, received a bad report that his kingdom was surrounded by their enemies, the Moabites and the Ammonites. Jehoshaphat knew that Judah didn't have a chance in its own might to win this battle, so he cried out to God for help. Read 2 Chronicles 20:1–31 through once to familiarize yourself with this passage, keeping in mind the words you looked up in day 1 and paying special attention to Jehoshaphat's actions after he received this bad report. Record your insights.

2. What was the first emotion Jehoshaphat felt according to verse 3, and where did he place his focus?

3. Jehoshaphat felt fear, but he did not allow that fear to paralyze him; rather, his fear motivated his faith to seek God. When something provokes fear in you, do you immediately take it to the Lord, or do you hold on to it, nurse it for a while, and begin to feel defeated?

4. From the scriptures you read in 2 Chronicles 20, in your own words, what did Jehoshaphat do after receiving the news of impending disaster that can help you the next time you face adversity?

5. Do you set yourself to seek the Lord for answers when impossible situations arise, or do you tend to use your own reasoning and understanding to find solutions?

6. According to Proverbs 3:5–6, what wise insight are we given about human understanding?

7. In 2 Chronicles 17, 18 and 19, we find the account of Jehoshaphat. He had riches and honor in abundance and became increasingly powerful, building fortresses all throughout Judah. He had armies of more than a million men, yet he did not trust his own wisdom and resources but looked to God. He was a man of great faith who put his trust in God. Read Psalm 20:6–8, where is the wrong place and the right place to put our trust?

8. In today's terms, what do you think chariots and horses might represent in our lives? Examine your life and ask God to help you identify anything in which you may be putting your trust other than Him. Record your insights.

9. Read 2 Chronicles 20:3–12 and record other ways Jehoshaphat's faith in action can be seen as he prepares Judah in seeking the Lord.

10. In verses 3–5, Jehoshaphat proclaimed a fast, and the people of Judah gathered together in the house of the Lord to seek Him. What does this tell you about the minds and hearts of Jehoshaphat and his people?

11. Jehoshaphat and the people of Judah were coming together in agreement—of one mind, unity, and of one accord. According to Matthew 18:19–20, what did Jesus say about the power of praying in agreement?

12. What does Jehoshaphat acknowledge about God in His prayer to God in verses 6–12?

13. What a powerful way to pray and praise God! Jehoshaphat acknowledges God's sovereign dominion and rule and His power and might. He reminds God of their covenant relationship and how the land was their promised possession. How do you think praying God's power and attributes, as

well as all that you possess in Christ, can strengthen your prayer and praise life and build up your faith in God?

14. According to verse 9, how determined was Jehoshaphat to have his prayers answered, and how do we see his faith declared in this verse?

15. How would you describe your prayer life? Are you determined to press on in prayer and praise until you see victory, or do you find yourself giving up before the victory is ever won?

16. What did Jehoshaphat confess to the Lord in verse 12?

17. Are you able to acknowledge your weakness and limitations to the Lord and ask for His help?

Power Meditation

"The angel of the Lord encamps
all around those who fear Him, and delivers them
Many are the afflictions of the righteous,
but the Lord delivers him out of them all" (Psalm 147:1)

Day 3: Praise Moves Us from the Battle to the Victory

Power Verse: "Now when they began to sing and to praise, the Lord set ambushes against the people of Ammon, Moab, and Mount Seir, who had come against Judah; and they were defeated." (2 Chronicles 20:22)

1. Read 2 Chronicles 20:13–30 to get familiar with this passage of Scripture. Record insights or questions that come to your mind concerning these verses.

2. In verses 14–17, how did God respond to Jehoshaphat's faith and his determination?

3. What a tremendous promise we have from God: that the battle is not ours but His. Are there areas in your life where you are trying to fight and win the battle instead of trusting God to fight and win the battle for you?

4. What instructions did God give the people in verse 17? What did He say their part in the battle would be?

5. God did not tell them just to stay in their tents and do nothing during the battle, but He said to go out to the battle, take their position, stand and not fear, and see the salvation of the Lord. What did their position involve and how did they prepare for the battle from Verse 20–21?

6. More than likely, in our lifetime, we will not have to go out to battle against flesh and blood. According to Ephesians 6:11–12, who do we battle in this life?

7. How are we to position ourselves and stand, according to Ephesians 6:13–18?

8. According to 2 Chronicles 20:18–19, how did Jehoshaphat and the people show thanksgiving to God for this answer to prayer?

9. If you were in a battle of this magnitude, do you think you would be able just to trust God and take Him at His Word? How much human reasoning and understanding do you think would come into play if this were a battle you were facing? Do you think you would at least want some armor on and a few guns with you—in case you heard God wrong?

   Many of us are constantly defeated by circumstances because we aren't ready to accept that the battle belongs to the Lord, not us. Even when we realize our own powerlessness to cope with the enemy, we are afraid to let go and trust ourselves to God's power. Could this be because we give the wrong priority to our own understanding? Do we say, "I don't understand; therefore, I don't believe?" Jehoshaphat would never have dared to follow God's plan for battle if he had insisted on understanding it first. Verse 20 says that Jehoshaphat was a man who believed God.

10. According to verse 22, at what point did they get the victory?

    Praise moves us from the battle to the victory. Jehoshaphat deliberately went into an impossible situation, carrying the shield of faith and the weapon of praise and watched God perform a miracle. Do you think God only performed miracles in the Old and New Testament? Do you believe God can perform miracles today? According to Hebrews 13:8, has God changed?

11. God not only destroyed and defeated Jehoshaphat's enemies, He also gave Jehoshaphat and his people all the valuables found on the dead enemies' bodies. Verse 25 says it took three days to carry away all the precious jewelry. According to Ephesians 3:20, what is God able to do for you and me, and how does He accomplish it?

12. How did Jehoshaphat and his people celebrate this tremendous victory in verses 27–28?

13. Read verse 30, what did God give to Jehoshaphat?

    How about you, beloved? Do you need God to give you rest? Let Him fight the battles of life for you so that you can enjoy peace and rest.

14. God wants us to be victorious Christians in this life. Every one of us have areas in which we want to see victory. Getting victory over sin is the biggest conquest we face each day. Praise the Lord, He has given us victory to overcome sin. How can 1 John 5:4–5, 1 Corinthians 15:57–58 and Romans 8:37 reinforce this truth in our hearts?

15. How has God spoken to you today?

Power Challenge

The next time you face a difficult challenge, remember King Jehoshaphat. Set yourself to seek the Lord. Encourage yourself in the Lord with His Word. Praise Him for how great and mighty He is and how nothing is impossible for Him. Stand in faith, firmly trusting and standing on God's promises. Take your position in Christ and in the power of His blood, and in the authority of His name, reject the devil's lies. The devil is a defeated foe. Remember that He who is in us is greater than he who is in the world and that the battle is not ours but God's. In the midst of adversity, choose to praise God and thank Him that He is in control, no matter what your circumstances may look like. Purpose in your heart that you will stand and see the salvation of the Lord. In Psalm 81:10, God says to open your mouth wide, and He will fill it. Ask Him to write a new song on your heart that you can sing back to Him. If we will do these things, we will be victorious every time. Praise the Lord!

Power Meditation

> "Blessed be the God and Father of our Lord Jesus Christ, who according to His abundant mercy has begotten us again to a living hope through the resurrection of Jesus Christ from the dead" (1 Peter 1:3).

Day 4: Praise: Power Unlimited

Power Verse: "And now my head shall be lifted up above my enemies all around me; therefore, I will offer sacrifices of joy in His tabernacle; I will sing, yes, I will sing praises to the Lord." (Psalm 27:6)

At times, there is deep sacrifice in praise. Sometimes, we must praise God through tears, pain, and suffering. I am sure there is nothing more precious to God than the praises that come from a life undergoing suffering. Praise lifts our eyes from our circumstances to our Almighty Father, who is Ruler over all things. Not one circumstance can come into our lives without His permission. Romans 8:28 tells us God has ways of causing our circumstances to work together for His glory and our good. Whatever situations you are facing today—many of which are not your own choosing—praise the Lord. Whenever the clouds of darkness begin to hide God's loving face, praise is the quickest way through to His glorious light again. Today, we will study God's Word to see how we can see His unlimited power at work when we choose to praise Him in the times of adversity.

1. Do you find it difficult to praise God when things aren't going smoothly?
2. Describe circumstances that have come into your life that have made it difficult for you to praise God.

3. The Apostle Paul was well acquainted with pain and suffering. He wrote three-fourths of the New Testament and was in the center of God's will, yet He suffered great hardships and persecution. Read 2 Corinthians 11:24–28 and list the hardships Paul encountered in his ministry.

4. Throughout the New Testament, Paul exhorts us to rejoice, be glad, and continually give thanks to God. Read Philippians 3:7–14. According to this passage, what things had Paul learned that caused him to be able to rejoice and give thanks to God in every circumstance?

5. Sometimes, we get the mistaken idea that if we are doing the work of the Lord and following His direction and will for our lives, that we should be free from hardships. Scripture does not teach that. Read Acts 16:16–33. What had Paul and Silas been doing that got them thrown into prison?

6. What kinds of abuse did they suffer in verses 22–24?

7. What was the attitude of Paul and Silas in the midst of their bad circumstances? According to verses 25–26, what was the result of their actions?

    The devil wanted them to feel hopeless and helpless in their situation. Paul and Silas knew the power of praise to God. Praise was all it took to break the chains that bound them and to open the prison door to their freedom. God didn't deliver them from prison, but through praise, delivered them in it.

8. What thinking, attitudes, or actions make you feel bound and chained in your own life from which you need God to deliver you?

    Are you willing to praise God where you are, thanking Him that He has the power to deliver you?

9. What do you think the other prisoners thought when they heard Paul and Silas sing praises to God?

10. Paul and Silas could have grumbled and complained in prison and felt totally mistreated. Instead, because they praised God and had an attitude of thanksgiving, they were

THE POWER IN THINKING GOD'S WAY

able to witness and give testimony to the other prisoners to the awesome power of God. Can you think of times when you have destroyed God's credibility to others by complaining?

11. What other miracle did God perform in this prison in verses 27–33?

God used Paul and Silas in a mighty way to accomplish His purpose. Many times God uses trials and hardships in our lives to make us be a witness to the lost. When we submit to God in those situations, trusting Him and praising Him, we will glorify Him, and the lost will see something different in our lives that they will want in their own lives.

12. In the midst of trials, do you allow God to use you as an instrument that will bring glory to Him and reach the lost? Do you have an attitude of gratitude, or are you prone to doubt God and complain?

13. What does Paul exhort us to do in 1 Thessalonians 5:16–18?

14. According to these verses, is it God's will for us to praise and thank Him only when things are going the way we want?

15. Since it is God's will for us to live in an attitude of prayer, an attitude of rejoicing, and an attitude of thanksgiving, where should we place our focus as a habit of life?

16. What does God want to change in you that would cause you to become a Christian who praises Him in spite of difficulties?

17. Read Philippians 4:10–13. What did hardships and difficulties teach Paul that can encourage us as we face hardships?

18. How has God spoken to you today?

Power Challenge

We can't change ourselves from unbelieving grumblers to thankful, cheerful believers. God has to do the changing. We must make the decision to stop complaining and start thanking and praising God, but it is God's power that works the transformation. Our job is to keep our eyes on Jesus and to thank God for what He is able to do. In practice, we will find that God will bring into our lives the very kinds of circumstances that used to trigger our complaining. When they come, we can thank and praise God because He is using those very things to bring about change in us. The things that used to make us grumble and stumble will prove to us God's strength and power and will serve to increase our faith. Learning to accept everything that happens with an attitude of thanksgiving will release the power of God in and through us, and we will soon be able to experience God's peace and joy.

Power Meditation

"But may the God of all grace, who called us to His eternal glory by Christ Jesus, after you have suffered a while, perfect, establish, strengthen, and settle you. To Him be the glory and the dominion forever and ever. Amen" (1 Peter 5:10–11).

Day 5: Praise: The Secret to Joy
Power Verse: "But now I come to You, and these things I speak in the world, that they may have My joy fulfilled in themselves." (John 17:13)

Jesus not only came to purchase our salvation, but He also came to provide us with the sustaining power of His joy. The amplified version of today's Power Verse says this: "That My joy may be made full and complete and perfect in them, that they may experience My delight fulfilled in them, that My enjoyment may be perfected in their souls, that they may have My gladness within them filling their hearts" (John 17:13, AMP). If Jesus came so that our joy would be complete and perfect in Him, why are so many Christians joyless? Is it because too many Christians walk by their feelings and not by faith? In our study of praise, we have already seen that praise involves an act of our will. When our will lines up, then our emotions and intellect follow. The same is true for us to be joyful. Jesus prayed that His joy would be fulfilled, or perfected, in us. We must choose to accept what Jesus has done for us and allow Him to perfect His joy in us. In practice, this means that we deliberately set out to practice joy, regardless of how we feel. We must trust that God will go to work, transforming our sorrows into joy, just as He promised. Joy is not triggered by our emotions but is a choice of our will and is part of a life of praise. Praise will activate joy in our lives, the kind of joy that rises above our circumstances and focuses on the character of God. The psalmist rejoiced in God's righteousness (Psalm 71:14–16), God's salvation (Psalm 21:1, Psalm 71:23), God's mercy (Psalm 31:7), God's creation (Psalm 148:5), God's Word (Psalm 119:14, 162), and God's faithfulness (Psalm 92:1–2). It is God's character and characteristics that cause us to rejoice. Our final day will be spent looking into God's Word to see how we can experience the power of the joy of the Lord in our lives every day.

1. Do you consider yourself a joyful person all of the time, most of the time, or hardly at all?
2. In your own words, how would you define joy?
3. Do you think joy and happiness are the same thing? Explain your answer.
4. Do your outward circumstances need to be free of problems in order for you to feel joyful?
5. Look up the definition for *joy* in your concordance or dictionary and record your insights. Feel free to use any other study materials you might have on joy.
6. According to Nehemiah 8:10, how do we overcome sorrow, and what is the source of our strength?
7. What do you think the differences are between the joy of the Lord and just feeling happy about something?
8. To have joy is to have gladness of heart, to be of good cheer, to be delighted, and to have a spirit of rejoicing within. It is a spiritual gladness, and it comes from the Lord. According to the following verses, where are the godly to find joy and gladness?

Psalm 32:11
Psalm 35:9
Psalm 64:10

Psalm 97:12
Psalm 104:33–34

The joy of the Lord is a holy, spiritual joy and is not carnal or sensual. It cannot be manufactured by the flesh. Perhaps, the reason Christians are missing out on the joy that Jesus came to complete in us is because we are looking for it in all the wrong places. We have adopted wrong thinking that says, "Unless everything is going smoothly in my life, I can't be happy and I can't experience joy." Our thinking has become conformed to the world's thinking and values. We are trying to find happiness and joy the same way the world is trying to find it. We will never enjoy the joy and gladness of heart that Jesus came to give us as long as we are more interested in enjoying the comforts and pleasures of this world. Would God call this comfortable Christianity "the Church of Laodicea?" Comfortable Christianity will lead to dead and dry religious activities that will be void of joy, strength, and power because the joy of the Lord is our strength (Revelation 3:14–22).

9. According to Galatians 5:22, what is the source of joy in the Christian life?

10. Are you bearing the fruit of joy in your life?

11. How do we abide in Jesus's love according to John 15:10?

12. According to John 15:11, why did Jesus speak these words to us?

The source of joy is not found in happy circumstances but in knowing Jesus's commandments and obeying them and abiding in Him. Joy is a fruit of the Spirit, produced by the Holy Spirit in us as we yield to His rulership in our lives. This type of joy looks beyond the present circumstances to God's goodness, knowing that He will cause things to work together for our good.

13. Have you experienced joy in your own life as you walk by the Spirit, obey the Word of God, and have chosen to rejoice when difficult situations arise?

14. The Apostle Peter knew we would experience trials and adversities. According to 1 Peter 4:12–14, what should our attitude be when we are going through trials?

15. Read Jeremiah 15:15–16. What was Jeremiah's source of joy and rejoicing through hardships?

16. Jeremiah delighted himself in the Word of God. It gave him joy and caused his heart to rejoice. What does God promise to give us when we delight ourselves in Him, according to Psalm 37:4?

    To have joy is to be happy, delighted, glad. It is an overflowing, pleasant experience. Joy does not depend on feelings. We are not to rejoice because we feel joyful; rather, we can expect to feel joyful as a result of rejoicing. The practice of praise and rejoicing will cultivate the joy already planted in us by the Holy Spirit.

17. Psalm 22:3 says that God inhabits the praise of His people. When we begin to praise God, His presence is near us. According to Psalm 16:11, what does God's presence bring to our lives?

18. What types of thinking and attitudes does the Lord want to change in you so that you can enjoy His sustaining power of joy to overflowing in your life?

19. Read Habakkuk 3:16–19. In verse 16, Habakkuk expresses his concerns over his present circumstances of Judah being invaded by the Babylonian army. What were his conclusions in verses 17–19 about how he would deal with this trouble?

20. Substitute your own circumstances and factors in verses 17 and 18 and write them out.

    Though
    nor
    though
    and
    though
    and
    yet I will

21. Rewrite verse 19 in your own words as your commitment to praise God and to become more joyful in spite of circumstances in your life.

Power Challenge

Is your spiritual life lacking joy? Be sure there is no hidden and unconfessed sin in your life, then simply start praising God. If you need a new fountain of joy to spring up inside your soul, praise God. The Word says that God puts a song in each one of our hearts. If we are not singing Christians, we are disappointing God. We don't have to wait to praise God for only grandiose things but also for the things we would otherwise take for granted. Waking up in the morning, being able to see, hear, smell, walk, talk, the ability to make decisions, driving to the grocery store—the list is endless. Perhaps, you have been sensing the Holy Spirit telling you that you need praise in your life. Confess it to God and ask Him to provoke within you an attitude of praise and thanksgiving every day. My challenge to you is to write a song from your heart, and then sing it to the Lord. See if you don't experience a new touch of His glory.

Power Meditation

"Lift up your heads, O you gates!
And be lifted up, you everlasting doors!
And the King of glory shall come in.
Who is this King of glory?
The Lord strong and mighty, the Lord mighty in battle.
Lift up your heads, O you gates!
And lift them up, you everlasting doors!
And the King of glory shall come in" (Psalm 24:7–9).

Beloved, we are the gates and doors. Lift up the gates of your hearts and the doors of your minds and lips, and praise God and the King of glory will come in.

Leader's Guide

The Power in Thinking God's Way

And do not be conformed to this world, but be transformed by the renewing of your mind, that you may prove what is that good and acceptable and perfect will of God.

—Romans 12:2, NKJV

Jackie Sciascia

About the Author
of the Leader Guide

Jackie Sciascia was called by the Lord to be a Barnabas, an encourager, to the author of *The Power in Thinking Gods Way*, Judy Golightly. Her spiritual gifts from the Lord are teaching and exhortation. The gospel was presented to her in high school in 1970 by a close family friend named Jack Archer. In 1990, she started her first precept study, followed by other precept courses. In 1992, she met Dr. Arnold Fruchtenbaum, a Messianic theologian who today is one of the foremost authorities on the nation of Israel. Dr. Fruchtenbaum, now a good friend, has taught Jackie to study and to apply the Jewish frame of reference and the Jewish traditions of the scriptures when studying the Biblical text. This has given her a greater appreciation of God's Word and a deeper affection for the Lord's beloved nation of Israel.

In 1994, the Lord brought Jackie and Judy together at a Women's Ministries meeting. Shortly thereafter, they discovered they had a lot in common. Both of them had lived in Dallas at the same time; both had taken precept courses and shared a love of studying God's Word; both were the oldest children in their families; each has one child, a daughter; and both are Martha's who long to become Mary's, sitting at the feet of Jesus and not at the feet of their problems.

Jackie has been married since 1979 to a wonderful husband, Charles Sciascia, who has given her unconditional love and support and a beautiful daughter, Lauren, who is a precious gift from the Lord. She also has a Shaklee business out of her home. The Lord has also blessed Jackie with a wonderful son in law Chris Nikkel and two beautiful grandsons, Everett & Silas.

Acknowledgments

Jackie would like to give special note of thanks to her parents, Mr. and Mrs. G. P. Falbo, for being wonderful parents and to her three wonderful sisters: Nancy Bruce, Gail Smith, and Sally Franklin, who also have a tremendous love for the study of God's Word. She is also grateful to her pastor, Dr. George Harris, and all the body of Christ at Castle Hills First Baptist who have prayed, helped, and given support to Judy Golightly while this study was being written. In addition, Jackie would like to thank Judy for her encouragement regarding the discussion guide and for all her prayers and support every week while this was being written. And finally, Jackie would like to express her appreciation to all her friends in the Lord who have encouraged her over the years to keep pressing on.

Guidelines for Small Group Discussion Leader

The leader's responsibility is to lead a discussion of the homework, not to teach it. Your goal, through the power of the Holy Spirit, is to discern and encourage your group to share their insights and revelations regarding each week's assignment. Prompt them to discuss how they felt the Holy Spirit used the material in the lesson to minister and reveal to them areas in their life requiring the Lord's attention.

The following are recommendations for leading a small group.

Depend upon the Holy Spirit and prayer to lead your group. "I will instruct you and teach you in the way you should go; I will counsel you with my eye upon you" (Psalm 32:8, NAS).

For home setting: Your small group should consist of eight to ten people.

For a classroom setting: If your group is larger than ten and less than 15-20, there will be no need to break into small groups.

Begin with prayer, taking any prayer requests the ladies may have at this time. Keep prayer requests short (this is not a prayer meeting; time is a factor).

Be the encourager; introduce yourself to your group, and tell them a little something about yourself before getting started. Provide a warm, comfortable atmosphere where all will feel free to share.

At the first session, go around the table and ask each person (calling them by name) to introduce themselves to the group. Name tags are very important to achieve this, so be sure each person has one. This is a good ice breaker, and it makes people coming together for the first time feel comfortable.

Make it a point during the course of this study to get to know one another. Exchange phone numbers, and pray for one another during the week. This makes for a more intimate setting.

Starting the Discussion Time

Each chapter of this study is broken down into five days of homework. Discussion time should be ten to 15-18 minutes per chapter, 75-90 minute group discussion.

Each day in the leader guide has an introductory paragraph designed to assist with discussion. Be sure to read the introductory paragraph of each day to your group.

There are a number of discussion questions for each day, choose two (or more if you wish), depending upon the leading of the Holy Spirit. Always ask your group what questions from the lesson they found interesting and encourage them to share their insights. Note that there will be questions from the homework and questions that are not from the study. Questions with a number next to them pertain to the lesson.

Do not get sidetracked and go off on tangents. Keep the discussion relevant to the homework and please, do not let any one person control the discussion time.

It is important to cover all five days of each chapter during the discussion time. This will motivate your group to complete their homework. Please encourage your group to do their homework each week. Only those who have persevered in completing the lessons may share. And please remember we want everyone to come each week even if their homework has not been completed!

Prayer, faithful completion of homework, and dependency on the Holy Spirit is a requirement to be an anointed leader. May the Lord be your strength, your hope, and your shield, and may his blessings abound on all of you who delight yourselves in his Holy Word.

Chapter 1
The Importance of Our Thought Life

Day 1: Think About What You've Thinking About!

Read to your group:

Do you see the importance of your thought life? *"For as he thinks in his heart, so is he"* (Proverbs 23:7 NKJ). "For as he reflects or intends or purposes in his heart, so he is." Do you really want to know the real you? Then what are you meditating on? If you want to know the condition of your heart, examine your thought life!

Question 2—Is he speaking of an organ? What do you think this verse means?

Question 4—What about what we become health wise? Proverbs 3:8; 4:22

Question: Are your thoughts the real you?

Day 2: Guard Your Thought Life!

Read to your group:

Why guard your thought life? Just as the heart is the center of the flow of life in your physical body, your thoughts are the center of your spiritual and emotional flow of life. That is why it is so important for us to protect and guard our thoughts because important life-changing decisions are made every day based upon what we have been meditating on.

Question 1—Discuss the definition.
Question 2—Why guard your mind/heart? And what does *the issues of life*" mean?

Go over the verses below and explain how our thoughts affect our lives!

Proverbs 12:25; Proverbs 13:12
Good results: Proverbs 14:30; Proverbs 15:13, 30

Question 5—How does Satan take Scripture and use it to bring confusion and disobedience into our lives?

Day 3: The Mind of Christ vs. the Mind of the Flesh

Read to your group:

Right thinking leads to right living. In order to have the mind of Christ, we must know his Word and more importantly, live it out. You can go to church and even take Bible studies, but you will never overcome the mind of the flesh without reading, memorizing, meditating, and most importantly, obeying the Word.

Question: What has to happen to your thought life in order for you to become more Christ-like?
Question: Look up the following verses and discuss the power of mediations: Psalms 1:2; Psalms 63:6; Psalms 119:48
Question 2—Give some examples of thoughts that produce life.
Question 4—What are thoughts that produce death? Give examples.
Question 10—Is it possible to go back and forth between spiritual thoughts and fleshly thoughts? Romans 7:15, 16, 20

Day 4: The Mind of Faith vs. the Mind of the Flesh

Read to your group:

The Lord wants us to walk by faith, not by flesh. Do you know the difference? Many Christians today do not know the difference because they are not in the Word. Instead of God's Word, their feelings become their measure of what is truth.

Question 1—Apply the definition of faith to the power verse.
Question: If faith comes by hearing, can fear come the same way?
Question 7—How hard is it to believe God for things you cannot see? What does "faith in faith" mean?
Question: Joshua and Caleb's faith didn't just suddenly happen. How was their walk with the Lord different than that of the other spies?
Question: Could you say that the Jewish people had put their confidence in fear?

The Israelites were supposed to take possession of the land. The word *possession* means ownership or occupation of.

Question: How can the flesh occupy or own your thought life?

Day 5: Right Thinking Will Lead to Right Praying

Read to your group:
When we read and study the Bible, God is the one who is speaking to us. When we pray, we are having communication with the Most High God of the Universe. Prayer is not an option; but a very important command. 1 Samuel 12:23 says: it is a sin if we do not pray for others. The following verses show the importance and power of prayer.

We pray without ceasing—1 Thessalonians 5:17
We pray steadfastly—Colossians 4:2
Prayer is necessary for victory—Ephesians 6:10–18

Question 1—Discuss the definition, and apply it to the power verse.
Question: How does belief affect your prayer life?
Question 5—How is unbelief disobedience?
Question: Read 1 Samuel 15:22–23. How does God view our disobedience?

Chapter 2
The Mind is the Battlefield

Day 1: Pick Up Your Weapons

Read these definitions to your group, and apply them to the homework questions:

Information: Knowledge obtained from investigation, study, or instruction.

Application: The act of putting to use.

Transformation: To change in character or condition. *Transform* implies a major change in form, nature, or function.

The act of studying God's Word and putting scripture to use will result in a major change in the character or condition of the form, nature, and function of the heart/mind.

Question 1—Why is it important to know where the war is taking place?

Question 2—What is the application of *"mighty in God?"*

Question 4—How can each of the above definitions be applied to verse 5?

The definition of *exalt* is to rise in rank, power, or character, to enhance the activity of.

Question 4, Part 2—In light of this definition, what does *"exalts itself against the knowledge of God"* mean to you?

Day 2: Bringing Thoughts Captive to the Obedience of Christ

Read to your group:

Stronghold means to fortify by holding safely or to defend a personal belief, idea, or opinion against outside opposition. We can use fear, ignorance, stubbornness, etc. to build walls around the lies we believe. The anorexic woman is an excellent example. Like her, we, too, will choose to defend the lies we believe.

Question: Give some examples of how you could defend or protect a lie in your life.

Question 1—What types of thoughts should we bring captive?

Question 2—Discuss the definition of *argument*. Using that definition, explain how we help ourselves to stay in bondage.

Question 7—Go over the definitions.

> *Captive:* Taken and held as a prisoner of war by an enemy in war, kept within bounds.
>
> *Obedient:* Compliant with the one who is in authority, docile, easy to handle, or manage.

Day 3: Armed and Dangerous

Read to your group:

As believers, we must always have our armor on. In order to be good soldiers of Christ, we must practice, practice, practice.

Practice: To train by repeated exercises to become proficient. *Practice* further implies the attainment of skill through much repetition.

Question 2—Being *"strong in the Lord"* denotes a continuous command. We must practice dependency on the Lord. We must practice going to him.

Using the definition of *practice*, how does it and *"strong in the Lord"* go together?

Question 3—Discuss the definition of *wiles*.

Question 4—Why do you think truth is the first piece of armor that we must put on?

Question 9—Why does God call for the heart to be covered and protected?

Day 4: Victory, Not Victims

Read to your group:

Sovereignty: Supreme power over authority, free from external control—autonomy.

God's Word has supreme power over all powers and principalities. The Lord reigns supreme over all our ups and downs, stresses, and cares. He never fluctuates so neither does his Word!

Question: Why is peace so important in our spiritual life?

Questions 3 and 4—Based on these two questions, what is the incentive for holy living?

Question 5—Who is the fire in 1 Corinthians 3:15? Look up Hebrews 12:29. Could the fire that we are walking through at the judgment seat of Christ be God himself?

Questions 7 and 9—What about the importance of faith in our battle? Faith is making a decision to trust, lean, or depend upon someone or something. If we do not have our shield up, who will we ultimately end up depending upon?

Day 5: The Privilege, Power, and Promise of Prayer

Read to your group:

When we study the Bible, God is speaking to us; but when we pray, we are speaking to him. Prayer is especially important to our spiritual health and vitality. It helps to keep us dependent on God, and it helps to keep the relationship alive.

Question 1—Describe the Word of God.

Question 2—Describe the power of the Word.

Question 4—The Word of God is our most powerful defense against Satan. Jesus is our example to follow in our warfare with the devil. What did Jesus do every time he was tempted?

Question: Do you believe we need to use specific scriptures for specific circumstances? Did Jesus?

Chapter 3
The Renewed Mind —
A Vital Necessity

Day 1: The Answer

Read to your group:

Trust: Assured reliance on the character, ability, strength, or truth of someone or something; one in whom confidence is placed.

It is important that the Word of God directs our thinking, but in order for that to happen, we have to trust or have assured reliance on the ability and truth of the awesome power of the Word. In essence, we have to trust it enough to want to apply it to our lives.

On the bottom of page fifty-seven, Judy says, "If there is no mind change, there will be no life change."

Question: How true is the above statement?
Question: How much confidence should we place in God's Word?
Question 5—Go over definitions: *world, conform, transform, renew,* etc.
Question 6—Applying the definitions above, what do you think Romans 12:2 is really saying?
Question: That which is conceived in the mind is carried out in the body. Do you agree that this is what Romans 12:1 could be saying?
Question: How are our thoughts carried out in the physical realm?

Day 2: A Surrendered Mind

Read to your group:

Confession of sin is not enough to help a believer automatically walk in the Spirit. The believer must become a yielded instrument for the service of God. This involves both the body and the mind, and a separation from the world's influence and control must happen before we can ever have victory in our lives.

Read Job 22:21 to group: "Yield now and be at peace with Him; thereby good will come to you" (NAS).

Question: According to this verse, how does yielding cause good things to happen in your life?

Question 1—Discuss the definitions of *surrender* and *submit.*

Question 2—What are we able to do with a surrendered will?

Question 8—To lean is the same thing as trust. Why is trusting or leaning on the flesh (which is our own understanding) so dangerous?

Day 3: Beware of Worldly Mindedness

Read to your group:

The key to a transformed life is in continuing to choose right thoughts. Without continuing to choose the right thoughts on a daily basis, Christians will soon experience defeat and will become friends with the world again. Remember, being friends with the world means being an enemy of God.

Question 2—*Pride* is self-confidence or dependence on self. Explain how not obeying God's Word can be prideful?

Question 3—Why is adultery used to describe friendship with the world?

Question 4—What are some examples of the tragic effects friendship with the world can produce in a believer's life?

Question 5—The world says dependence on self shows strength. God says when you are weak, then you are strong (2 Corinthians 12:10). How does weakness equal strength?

Day 4: Putting On the Mind of Christ and Putting Off the Mind of the Flesh

Read to your group:

The mind of Christ is his Word. If you do not know his Word, you will never have the mind of Christ. Salvation is just the beginning of the long road to renewal. This work is said to be accomplished through a lifetime of renewing the mind. Man's mind has been darkened by sin and must be brought to the place where it thinks as God thinks. This can only be accomplished through constant meditation on the Word of God (Psalms 1:2) and prayer.

Question 3—Discuss the description of eagles.
Question 5—Discuss the definition of *soar.*

The word of God holds us up, causing us to glide, soar, tower above our circumstances. But how are we able to do this? Read John 15:7, "If you abide in Me, and My words abide in you, ask whatever you wish, and it shall be done for you" (NAS).

Question: What is the key word in this verse?

Abide is the key word. It means to endure without yielding, withstand, to remain stable, to bear patiently. This is how one is able to soar, glide, etc.

Question 11—Contrast the two types of wisdom and give examples.

Day 5: Quit Deceiving Yourself

Read to your group:

Do you believe that all you need to be victorious is knowledge? How much do you need? Yes, God's word is powerful, and it can change lives, but we have to truly want that change enough to put the Word into practice in our lives.

Practice: To train by repeated exercises, to become proficient. Practice implies the attainment of skill through much repetition.

Question 3—*Implant* means teaching that makes for permanence of what is taught. Apply this definition to question 3.

Question 4—Which seed best describes your walk with the Lord?

Question 12—How does one become a doer of God's word? What keeps you from becoming a doer (remember: trust is involved with being a doer).

Chapter 4
Practicing the Truth of Who I Am in Christ

Day 1: God's Grace

Read to your group:

Is your search for significance and favor with God based upon a prescribed ritual? How well we perform today could determine our self-esteem tomorrow—is that the way our walk should be? Is your walk based upon faith or self-esteem? If your walk is based upon self-esteem, then everything must be earned and worked for. The approval you yearn for comes as a direct result of how productive and successful you are in the world's system and not as a result of the love and approval of God. We must walk by faith, not by self-esteem or the praises of men!

Question 5—*Justified* means just as we had never sinned. Is that hard to understand, or to believe?

Question: Why is it easier to accept a ritual or performance-based walk than a faithbased walk?

Question: Can you see the pressure and stress a performance-based walk can bring a believer?

Question: Why must we have the praises of men instead of the Word of God as our reassurance?

Day 2: I Am a New Creation in Christ

Read to your group:

Even after we are saved, we have an affinity for the world's values because the flesh is still with us. Every day we must check for thoughts and behaviors that have the propensity for worldly influence. We must believe we really are a new creation in Christ, and this does not happen without lots of practice!

Question 4—Why is it so hard for Christians to believe they really are new creatures?

Question 11—Do you have a hard time thinking of yourself as holy?

Question 12—Review with your group their position in Christ.

Day 3: Jesus, "The Author and Finisher of Our Faith"

Read to your group:

What keeps you going when times are difficult and hard? When things look bleak, what do you do? Satan wants us to give up; he wants to wear us down. Because he blew it, he wants us to blow it as well. Satan cannot steal your salvation, but he can steal your rewards! He would like us all to get nothing but wood, hay, and stubble at the Berna Seat of Christ! He knows that perseverance brings a wonderful prize for the runner of the race, and he is out to steal your special honor ladies!

Question 2—According to 1 Corinthians 9:27, what does it mean to be disqualified from the race? Can our disobedience cause us to be disqualified?

Questions 5 and 6—Apply the definitions from question five to running the Christian race.

Day 4: The Race

Read to your group:

The Holy Spirit once spoke to my heart and told me, "Do not pray what you see, but pray what God is able to do." Israel, when she saw what she would have to overcome in order to take the promised land, gave up. She forgot what God was able to do for her, and her unbelief caused her to go backward. As Judy says in day four, "Faith moves us forward; unbelief moves us backward."

Question 1—Judy made a good point in part two of question one:
   Have you ever thought you might be running someone else's race?

Question 7—Go over definitions.

Question 9—Apply definitions of question seven to our attitudes during trials.

Question: Does joyful mean that a trial is fun and a good time, or that the joy comes from knowing that the Lord is there with you, and he is going to get you through this time of testing and tribulation?

Day 5: Our Reward for Running the Race with Endurance

Read to your group:

Do you have a microwave mentality? Do you shift from waiting on God to the god of self for your solutions? Do you feel like people are looking at you asking, "Well what are you going to do about this?" and you are thinking, "I better come up with a solution quick or what will people think?" Sometimes the pressure from our family and friends can cause us to lose our dependency on God and return to dependence on self for a quick and painless decision. As Judy says in the homework, "Don't fall into the trap by thinking you must find your own way when hardships come." Self hates waiting on God!

Question 7—Have you ever felt like God has forgotten you?

Question 8—James says there is a specific reward for enduring a trial. What is it?

Question: Does knowing that there are specific crowns affect your walk in any way?

Chapter 5
Exposing Stinking Thinking

Day 1: Laying Aside Bitterness

Read to your group:

Thoughts are unspoken words! Could the language of your thought life stand the scrutiny of a microphone? If everyone could hear your thoughts, what would your feelings be right now? Well, someone is hearing your thought life every minute of every day, and that someone is the Lord.

Question 1—Discuss the definition.
Question: Could someone's negative words about you be a result of their own defilement?
Question 5—Discuss the definition.
Question 6—Hebrews 12:15 says many are defiled. What does the word *many* mean? How many lives are defiled forever by our words? Example: What would the negative results be in telling a young child he's dumb and can't learn?

Day 2: Freedom from a Life of Strife

Read to your group:

Strife: Bitter, sometimes violent, conflict, or dissension; an act of contention, fight, struggle; exertion or contention for superiority.

Today's lesson is freedom from strife. As you can see from the above definition, strife is the total act of surrendering to the authority and control of the flesh. The flesh must have its way, and everyone must agree with it. Strife brings division in households, splits congregations, and eventually causes relationships with friends and family to come to an end. All the answers for strife are found in the scriptures, and knowing the Word will give us the discernment and wisdom we need to avoid strife in our lives.

Question: Why is total separation sometimes the only solution to strife?
Question 3—According to 1 Corinthians 3:1–4, where were these men placing their trust?
Question 9—What blessing is promised in 1 Peter 3:10?
Question 10—Discuss the definitions.

Day 3: Envy and Jealousy–The Twin Sins

Read to your group:
Envy and jealousy are very powerful emotions. Left unchecked, they can bring total destruction to friends and family and even co-workers. Jealousy and envy cause us to become totally corrupted in our thinking, and therefore our motives for everything we do must be examined closely.

Proverbs 16:2 (NAS) puts it like this, "All the ways of a man are clean in his own sight, but the Lord weighs the motives."

Question 1—Discuss the definitions.
Question 6—How does it make you feel to read in James 3:14–16 that envy in our hearts may be demonic?
Question 9—How do we as Christians make provisions for the flesh?

Day 4: The Poison and Passion of Anger and Wrath

Read to your group:
Do you know a person whose uncontrolled anger has totally destroyed their life? Have they viewed help or counseling with con-

tempt? The Lord tried to counsel Cain by telling him that "sin is crouching at the door; and its desire is for you, but you must master it" (NAS). Cain obviously did not listen to the Lord's wisdom; he chose to punish and to get revenge. As a result of his decision, sorrow and sadness followed him for the rest of his life.

Question 1—Discuss the power of uncontrolled anger according to Genesis 4:1–6.
Question 5—In verse 7, God tells Cain that sin is desiring him. How can sin desire us?
Question 10—According to Proverbs 21:19 and Proverbs 25:23–24, how can a wife's anger produce an unhappy home life?
Question 15—Explain how uncontrolled emotions can be so destructive in our thought life.

Day 5: Quit Judging and Criticizing

Read to your group:

The topic of judging is always a touchy subject among the Body of Christ. Matthew 7:1–5 is sometimes used by the world to teach that believers should never judge or even rebuke sin, of any kind, no matter how bad. They quote this scripture as proof, even though the word *sin* is not used in the passage. This kind of teaching violates all the other passages in the Old and New Testament where we are told to discern and to judge sin. In the New Testament we are told, "All Scripture is inspired by God and profitable for...reproof, for correction" (2 Timothy 3:16, NAS). We are admonished to "reprove, rebuke...with great patience..." (2 Timothy 4:2, NAS); "with gentleness correcting those who are in opposition..." (2 Timothy 2:25, NAS); and "if any among you strays from the truth, and one turns him back, let him know that he who turns a sinner from the error of his way will save his soul from death, and will cover a multitude of sins" (James 5:19–20, NAS).

In 1 Corinthians 5:1–8, excommunication of a local member was threatened if they were not brought to repentance. Finally, we are asked in 1 Corinthians 5:12 (NAS), "Do you not judge those who are within the church?" Matthew 7:1–5 talks about being very careful to examine and clean up our own lives first before we attempt to try to judge or rebuke another person about their attitudes, motives, struggles, faults etc.

Question 1—Discuss the definitions.
Question 2—Give examples of the kinds of reaping that a judgmental attitude can bring?
Question 7—Why do we fault others for the exact same sins we ourselves have?

Chapter 6
Recognizing Wilderness Mindsets

Day 1: The Rebellious and Stubborn Mindset

Read to your group:

Wilderness: Waste, an empty or pathless area or region.

What a destructive decision not to obey God! Demanding our own way and not trusting God with our lives could very well result in years of a wasted, empty, and a pathless life. Do you know people who have never learned what God is trying to teach them? Doesn't history always seem to be repeating itself, with the same old problems visiting them time and time again? Does the Lord keep allowing the same trial to come into your life over and over again, until you finally learn the lesson he's been trying to show you? Yes, he does!

Question 1—Go over the definitions and discuss how these attributes lead us to a wasted, empty, and pathless life!
Question: Why does God sometimes finally let us have our own way?
Question 14—What was the purpose of the manna, and what did God want to accomplish with it?
Question: Give an example by today's standards of full stomachs and empty hearts.

Day 2: The Complaining Mindset

Read to your group:

Did you ever really think that complaining about your life really might be complaining against God? Complaining is disobedience, and it kept the Israelites from the promised land and the rest and peace for which they longed. There is no peace for the one who complains because they are too busy looking at everything in their life that is wrong!

So remember Judy's admonition to us in the lesson: "Complaining is to the devil what praise is to God!"

Question 1—Go over the definitions, and discuss how you think they affect one's peace and rest!

Question 5—When a brother is suffering unjustly, what can we do to keep him encouraged?

Questions 9 and 10—Discuss.

Question 15—How can taking your complaints to the Lord make you feel better?

Day 3: The Forgetful Mindset

Read to your group:

Do you suffer from amnesia the way the Israelites did? When the Lord has answered your prayers over and over again, and then a new trial comes on the scene, do you become fearful and forget the faithfulness of the Lord? You are not alone. We need to do what David did in the Psalms: bring back to remembrance over and over again the faithfulness of God in passed trials and tribulations.

Question 1—How do these definitions apply to the forgetful mindset?

Questions 2–5—How can these questions be applied to our nation today?

Question 9—Name the false gods of this century.

Day 4: Minding the Past

Why does the past always look better when we are tested? "The good old days" weren't so good for the Israelites when they were in them. They longed to be set free but with their freedom came adjustments and a new way of living.

The past looked good to Israelites because of the security of knowing the Egyptians provided for their needs. It's strange to think that Israel would rather have had the pain of the past than the freedom of their present! They were so afraid of the unknown, even with God leading them, that they preferred going back into the slavery of Egypt. The freedom they desired put them in bondage and slavery to fear!

Question 2—How does God want us to deal with our past? Why are we told to forget the past?

Question 5—How do we let our past experiences affect our present and future?

Question 10—What is your insight into Psalms 51 and 32 regarding your past?

Day 5: The Mindset of Discontentment

Read to your group:

Discontentment comes when we compare our lives to others. For the last several decades, our nation's philosophy of excess as being the way and the truth and the life has caused us to never be satisfied, happy or—most of all—content with what we have. If you said to anyone you were content, people would assume you were just lazy and not ambitious enough! We must remember the flesh is never content, so give up trying to satisfy it; it will never happen! Turn your wants and desires over to the Lord, and let him tell you what is enough for you!

Question 1—Discuss the definition.

Questions 5 and 6—Discuss.

Question 17—Discuss the proper view of wealth through the scriptures given in homework.

Chapter 7
Overcoming a Martha Mentality

Day 1: The Worried Mind

Read to your group:

Abundant: Abounding, plentiful; an ample or overflowing quantity; affluence or wealth.
Abide: To remain stable or fixed in a state.

What does it mean to have an abundant life? What did Jesus mean when he said in John 10:10, "I came that they may have life, and might have it abundantly" (NAS). According to the above definition, the Lord intended for us to have an ample or overflowing quantity of his peace and a wealth of his joy! The abundant life is not speaking of the material world, but the spiritual one, which is abiding in him. He is the abundant life! We need to remember to remain in him.

Worry removes the abundant life and erases the promises of God from our minds. The peace and joy that is ours can be found nowhere else. Prayer and abiding in the scriptures, not your problems, is key to having the abundant life. You will either bow the knee and be at the feet of your problems, like Martha, or at the feet of Jesus, like Mary! Ladies, choose the good part as Mary did; be at the feet of Jesus.

Question 4—Why do you think Jesus asks us not to worry about food, clothing, or even tomorrow?
Question 7—How much time do you spend worrying about tomorrow?

Question 11—How has the enemy stolen gifts of peace and joy which the Father has sent to you?

Question 16—Discuss this if you have time.

Day 2: The Anxious Mind

Read to your group:

Anxiety in the heart of a man causes depression, but a good word makes him glad. Why does the heart respond to a good word? Could the Word of God be the medication our heart needs? Our hearts were created by the Lord to respond to the written and spoken Word of God. We were created by the Word, John 1:1, and we are healed by the Word. Matthew 8:5–13 tells us the centurion's servant was healed by the spoken Word of God. The scriptures themselves are anti-anxiety, calming our fears and anxious thoughts. Therefore, sow the Word of God in your hearts, and expect a more peaceful, worry free life!

Question 3—Your heart was created by God to respond to his words. Describe what the listed scriptures do to your heart.

Question 5—Describe the side effects of anxiety.

Question 7—How hard is it to totally surrender your problems to the Lord?

Question 12—What can we learn from David's prayer regarding overcoming anxiety?

Day 3: The Busy and Distracted Mind

Read to your group:

Satan's greatest deception and snare today is busyness. We are so busy that we do not have time for God, and no time for God equals: no power, no wisdom, no understanding, no discernment, no growth, no maturity, no rest, no peace, and no joy! In other words, you're of no use to the Kingdom of God! So of course Satan wants us busy. According to Galatians 1:10, we need to be careful that our works are not a result of us seeking favor with men! Are you saying yes to everything and everyone to please men? "I better say yes, because what will they think if I don't?" Does this sound anything like you? Well, let me remind you that your works will be revealed at the judgment seat of Christ, and if the foundation for all those works was not Christ but the flesh, then get ready for some wood, hay, and stubble!

Question 1—Discuss the definitions and relate how they affect our relationship with God.

Question 3—Name the warning signs of a far too-busy lifestyle and make application of those signs to your own life.

Questions 8 and 9—Describe how the judgment seat of Christ is a good motivator for evaluating our works!

Question 18—Describe the benefits of being quiet that are listed in the given scriptures.

Day 4: Overcoming the Legalistic and Self-Righteous Mind

Read to your group:

There can be arrogance and pride in legalism. Keeping the rules can puff us up and give us a haughty spirit. According to Psalm 138:6b, the Lord does not draw close to a person with a haughty spirit, because the verse states "but the haughty he knows from afar" (NAS). We are not closer to God because of the rules we keep but because of Christ, our Savior. You do not need a relationship with the Lord if you are going to live by a set of rules and regulations. In fact, you may not even know him very well or not at all, according to Isaiah 29:13, "Then the Lord said, 'Because this people draw near with their words and honor Me with their lip service, but they remove their hearts far from Me, and their reverence for Me consists of tradition learned by rote'" (NAS).

Do you have a tradition with God or a relationship with him? Is keeping the rules more important to you than the rule maker himself? Let's do as Judy admonishes us in the lesson: let's overcome living in legalism and discover the joy of living in God's grace.

Question 6—Go over this question and read the paragraph that follows.

Question 7—Describe different religious codes people might use to win God's approval.

Question 11—Do your dos and don'ts make you feel more righteous?

Question 14—What is the problem with putting your confidence in the flesh?

Day 5: The Controlaholic

Read to your group:

Are you a controlaholic? Do you consider yourself to be the general manager of your universe and everyone else's? Controlaholics put their confidence in the flesh and in their own ability and power to do what needs to be done. Letting go is not an option—it never enters their minds. Job 22:21 says, "Yield now and be at peace with Him; thereby good will come to you" (NAS).

What do you think the good is that the scripture is referring to? Maybe it is the peace, rest, and joy of knowing that you are not responsible for solving the world's problems because the solution to everything is Christ?

Question 2—How does being a controlaholic rob you of peace and joy?

Question 6—List the ways we can lean on our own understanding.

Question 11—How does Psalm 127:1–3 help to give us the right perceptive?

Question 13—Discuss the definition of *vain.*

Chapter 8
Do You Suffer with ITD (Impaired Thinking Disorder)?

Day 1: Are You Suffering from a Double Mind

Read to your group:

Doubt: To lack confidence in, distrust, an inclination not to believe.
Doubtful: Questions the worth, the honesty, or validity of a subject.

Are you able to discern a thought that is not from your heavenly Father? Do you know the difference between thoughts of the world/flesh and thoughts of the Spirit? Doubt can diminish the ability and the power to judge correctly what is from God and what is not. It causes a lack of confidence in the Word, and the result is an unstable roller-coaster walk with God. The flesh, with all its emotional highs and lows, becomes the standard by which we measure truth, instead of the scriptures. Truth is marred by doubt.

This is why it is so important for us to know God's thoughts: so we can have the ability to recognize when the devil is using our own thoughts to lie to us!

How has doubt diminished the ability for discernment in your life, especially when it comes to a decision which must be made?

Question 3—The power of the Word and faith in that Word caused Peter to walk above the storm. Give examples of how the scriptures have helped you to walk above the storms in your own life.

Questions 12–14—Describe the fruits of a doubter and the results of those fruits?

Question 17—Describe the power of faith in the listed verses. What point was our Lord trying to make through these scriptures?

Day 2: Fear Not

Read to your group:

Fear is Satan's source of power, just as faith is God's source of power in your life. Faith comes by hearing the Word of the Lord and acting upon it. Fear comes by hearing the word of the world, the flesh, and the devil, and acting upon it. Fear is fed through our minds into our spirits, resulting in debilitating, paralyzing thoughts. Totally forgetting God's Word, you will succumb to fears and its devastating effects.

Don't forget that over sixty-three times in the scriptures, God has told us not to fear. God wants us to walk believing and meditating on his Word and not believing and meditating on our problems and fears. We need to do what the Word commands us to do: "Walk by faith, not by sight" (2 Corinthians 5:7, NAS).

Question 3—Explain the timing of fear according to Genesis 3:6–10.

Question 8—Name the fruit produced in our lives when we walk by fear instead of faith?

Question 11—Discuss the power of faith in the verses listed.

Question 12—What do the listed verses tell us about freedom from fear?

Day 3: Inconsistent Thinking and Behavior

Read to your group:

Inconsistent: Not compatible with another fact or claim, changeable, illogical in thought and action.

When you live your life vacillating between the word and the world, the result for a believer will be an inconsistent walk with God. Our emotions change from day to day, but the Word of God is always the same; it never changes. Stability and the Word go hand in hand. Remember, the Lord wants us to be consistent in our walk and faithful stewards for his kingdom. The wise and steadfast usage of our time, gifts, and talents for the Lord will someday result in praise from our Father, "Well done, good and faithful servant."

Questions 3 and 4—Why are we so inconsistent when it comes to our tongues?

Question 7—Peter walked, talked, and lived with Jesus for three years, yet he denied him three times. Explain Peter's bitter response in verse 74 and the power of fear played in his response.

Question 15—What keeps you from being a consistent servant?

Day 4: Controlling the Tongue

Read to your group:

Jesus said in Matthew 12:34 that out of the abundance of the heart the mouth speaks. Our speech lets the world know our hearts. Our tongues have the power to direct our lives and the lives of others. Proverbs 18:21 says, "Death and life are in the power of the tongue, and those who love it will eat its fruit" (NAS). Your words bear much fruit, good, or evil. The Word of God in John 6:63 states that his words are life! We can speak death with our tongues or life! Learn to speak "life words" to one another, and let God's wonderful grace become a wellspring for your tongue so that its speech may give life!

Question 2—Discuss the power of the tongue in James 3:1–8 and its effects.

Questions 8 and 9—Give some examples of the fruit produced by a negative tongue.

Question 18—How can these verses help us to control our tongues?

Day 5: Mastering My Mouth

Read to your group:

Do you watch the words you speak? Our words have such power; we must be very watchful not to dwell on the negative side of life, or the negative will become our truth.

The strongholds in our lives are set in place by our words. Our words are power containers—natural, fleshly, carnal—ready to destroy on a moment's notice. Since our words have such tremendous power, we need to get our words lined up and in agreement with the Word of God! The Holy Spirit will help us to control our tongues, but we must be under the control of the Holy Spirit, not under the control of our tongues!

Question 2—How does our tongue reveal the value of one's religion?

Question 7—How did the bad word given in Numbers 13 and 14 negatively impact the children of Israel?

Question 11—What bad reports do you believe about yourself because of someone's word about you?

Question 19—Discuss what these scriptures have to say about our mouths!

Chapter 9
A Victor—Armed and Dangerous

Day 1: Praise—An Act of the Will

Read to your group:

We are told in the Scriptures that it is God's will that we praise him (Psalms 50:23, Isaiah 43:21, 1 Thessalonians 5:18). Psalms 149:6 says that we should "let the high praises of God be in [our] mouth and a two-edged sword in [our] hand" (NAS). Apparently, praise is so powerful, it can fight our battles. The Lord's strength and power are always present, but they become visibly manifested in our lives when we praise him. To praise God is to acknowledge who he is. This is done by meditating on all his attributes and declaring the excellent greatness of his glory in prayer.

Question 1—Discuss the definitions, and apply them to your time of praising the Lord.

Question 6—Should praise be a continuous action?

Question 8—After reading Psalms 42:11 and 43:5, explain how you think praise affects our moods and can even remove depression.

Question 9—Describe how praise has lifted you out of the pit.

Day 2: Prayer–Faith in Action

Read to your group:

"For the battle is not yours but God's" (2 Chronicles 20:15, NAS). How comforting to realize that in everything we face *in* our Christian life that we are not alone; he is with us. More importantly, he does all the fighting and defending for us if we just surrender to him. In all our circumstances, he truly is our way, our truth, and our life!

Question 1—Describe what you learned about praise after reading about King Jehoshaphat in 2 Chronicles 20:1–31.

Question 7—How many times has leaning on your own understanding gotten you into trouble in your Christian walk?

Question 15—How does the words, *"the battle is not yours but God's,"* make you feel regarding trials?

Day 3: Praise Moves Us from the Battle to the Victory

Read to your group:

"You need not fight in this battle; station yourselves, stand and see the salvation of the Lord on your behalf..." (2 Chronicles 20:17, NAS). This life the Lord has given us is not ours but his. All your struggles and battles in this life belong to him. We need to remember to stand before the throne and give God our whole life so we can see the salvation of the Lord on our behalf.

Question 1—According to verses 13–30, what mighty things happen when we surrender our battles to the Lord?

Question 5—According to verses 20–21, what pieces of spiritual armor were they wearing at the moment?

Question 9—What thoughts keep you from letting go and trusting God?

Question 10—According to verse 22, discuss the awesome power of praise.

Day 4: Praise–Power Unlimited

Read to your group:

Praise lifts our eyes from our circumstances to our Almighty Father, who is ruler over all things. Praise gives us supernatural peace, strength, and joy. It is the most wonderful medicine for a weary soul, a healing tonic. Praise is the antithesis of what we feel is natural.

Never lean on your own understanding when it comes to praise, or you will never do it during difficult times. Today, we will learn the result of praise in times of adversity.

Question 3—According to 2 Corinthians 11:24–28, why does God allow us to go through adversity? What would you say to those who teach that all suffering is usually a result of sin in our lives? How is this kind of teaching false according to 2 Corinthians 11!

Question 10—How did the power of praise bring the Philippian jailer to salvation?

Day 5: Praise—The Secret to Joy

Read to your group:

Why are so many Christians joyless? Could it be because we walk by our feelings instead of our faith? Could it be a problem with our relationship with the Lord? Or has our conformity to the world's system robbed us of our joy? Today's lesson focuses on joy and how to have more of it through the teachings of the scriptures.

Question 7—What is the difference between the joy of the Lord and happiness?

Question 8—What do these verses tell us about where our focus should be. Do you think focus is the secret to joy?

CPSIA information can be obtained
at www.ICGtesting.com
Printed in the USA
LVHW032232230122
709135LV00004B/182